Whole Wheat Banana Bread (2 loaves)
350° 50-60 min.

3c whole wheat flour
2c sugar
2c mashed bananas
1/2 c chopped nuts
2/3 c vegetable oil
2t baking soda
1t salt
1/2 t baking powder
4 eggs

Combine all & pour into greased (bottom only) pans.

· THE GREAT BOOK OF ·

BREAD

PHOTOGRAPHY by Peter Barry
ILLUSTRATIONS by Sally Brewer

DESIGNED by Julie Smith. Jacket designed by Heather Blagden
EDITED by Kate Cranshaw and Jillian Stewart

CLB 4424
© 1996 CLB Publishing

This edition published in 1996 by Smithmark Publishers, a division of U.S. Media Holdings, Inc.,
16 East 32nd Street, New York NY 10016

SMITHMARK books are available for bulk purchase for sales promotion and premium use.
For details write or call the manager of special sales,
SMITHMARK Publishers, Inc., 16 East 32nd Street, New York, NY 10016; (212) 532-6600

Produced by CLB Publishing
Godalming Business Centre
Woolsack Way, Godalming, Surrey, UK

ISBN 0-8317-1017-9

Printed in Singapore
10 9 8 7 6 5 4 3 2 1

· THE GREAT BOOK OF ·
BREAD

Rosemary & Nick Moon

SMITHMARK

Contents

Introduction

One of the most seductive and mouthwatering aromas on earth is that of freshly baked bread. Not only is it comforting and stimulating, but when the bread is homemade and the aroma is coming from your own kitchen, the final moments of anticipation are mingled with the most enormous satisfaction that you have created this tantalizing food.

Anyone can make bread. At its most basic it is merely a case of mixing flour and water together to form a rough dough which is then cooked to produce a flat bread. Man has been baking bread ever since he relinquished a nomadic lifestyle and settled down to grow crops – the earliest cultivated grains included wheat, spelt (a type of wheat), barley and rye, all of which were used to produce bread. It was the ancient Egyptians who perfected the art of bread-making and began experimenting with sourdoughs to raise or leaven the bread, thus making it more palatable than flat bread and opening up a whole new era of experimentation with bread.

Of course there are breads which require careful weighing and mixing to achieve the correct texture and consistency, but most basic mixtures need almost deliberate sabotage if they are to fail! So contrary to what many people believe bread making is for everyone, not least because it is one of the most satisfying tasks in the kitchen.

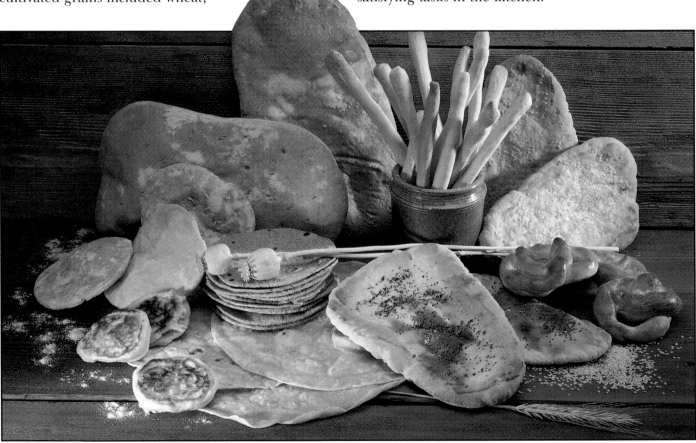

Clockwise from left to right: Ciabatta, Bread Sticks, Naan Breads, Pretzels, Naan Breads, Tortillas, Chapatties, Blinis, Pita Bread.

Basic bread-making equipment, including a tiny whisk for mixing yeast liquids, our handyman's knife kept specifically for slashing doughs, and a traditional dough scraper with our cheese cutter-cum-dough scraper.

The real bread revival

Fashions in bread change rapidly but it has always played an important part in the daily diet, providing plenty of fiber and carbohydrate. For years there was little interest in bread – it was just everyday, boring fare – but now, in common with so many other foods, the art of bread making is enjoying a real revival as more and more people discover just how many varied and interesting doughs may be made quite simply at home.

Equipment required for bread making

There is very little special equipment that you actually need for bread making, but there are a few things that will make the task easier for you.

A selection of mixing bowls is essential. You will need one large bowl for batch mixing of everyday breads, and a smaller bowl for more specialist or occasional

mixes, where you will be making just one loaf at a time. Purists would suggest china or glass bowls and we certainly agree that a china bowl seems to have the right homey qualities for bread making, but a plastic bowl with a cover often seems more reliable when it comes to keeping a dough at a constant temperature during proofing.

A sharp serrated-edged knife is a good alternative to a razor blade when scoring doughs prior to baking – we actually use a handyman's multipurpose knife, having carefully washed all the grease from the blade! Do remember to keep such a knife in the knife drawer with the blade guard in place, and not in the tool box for general use!

We have another tool which is always to hand, a dough cutter and scraper. This is a broad blade, not necessarily very sharp, in an easy-to-grip wooden handle. We use it to scrape up dough from the work surface during mixing (hence it must not be sharp, otherwise it might scratch) and also to cut the dough into portions. We have improvised and used a cheese cutter, left over from the days when we owned a delicatessen – catering suppliers should have the purpose-made tool though, or look out for a kitchen antique in a household sale.

Professional bakers use a flour thermometer for bread making, to ensure that all ingredients are at the optimum temperature before mixing commences. This is because they do not have the time to wait for doughs to reach temperature during the very tight schedule they have to adhere to with their ovens. For people like us, who make bread for enjoyment and satisfaction, a thermometer is not required – an extra ten minutes here or there during the bread making process will not matter at all.

You will require a variety of baking sheets and bread pans although you should never panic if you don't have exactly the correct size of pan called for in a recipe for everyday breads – dough in a deeper, narrower pan will just take a little longer to cook. However, the correct pan size is crucial for some of the enriched doughs for a classic presentation of these loaves.

Bread definitely benefits from being cooled quickly, and wire racks are best for this task. If you intend to do batch baking you will require two or three racks – if you run out of cooling space, look in your broiler pan, there's usually a spare wire rack in there!

Mixing by hand or machine

If you are busy in the kitchen a food mixer really comes into its own as it will take over the mixing and kneading of the dough for you. However, purists would scorn such assistance, preferring a totally hands-on approach so that they can feel the texture of the dough at every stage and react accordingly. My husband Nick falls into this category of bakers! He was baking when we first met and, as now, was producing the most delicious bread. After a hard day at the office he found baking a most enjoyable way to relax and let off steam, kneading the dough by hand and allowing it to benefit from the pent-up emotions brought home from his desk! I came to bread making from a completely different direction. As a home economist in a test kitchen I had to make bread to test ovens and, making six or eight loaves at

A small example of the variety of home-baked breads. From left to right: Baguette, Three-day Sourdough, *French Stick, Pumpernickel, Poppy Seed and Anchovy Focaccia, Moon's Whole-wheat Loaf, Soft Brown Rolls, Bath Buns, Bee'* *and Onion Bread, Burger Buns, White "Split" Loaf, Oatmeal Bread, Croissants, Morning Rolls, Zucchini Bread.*

a time, the food mixer was a necessary tool. My next job was with a food mixer manufacturer, so my dough hook was virtually a part of my right hand!

After years of bread making we are now coming to some joint decisions as to how it should be done! Without doubt it is best to mix the dough by hand – this really enables you to judge the mixture and to add extra flour or liquid as required. For personal satisfaction (and forearm muscle development!) it is therefore preferable to knead by hand but I can often be tempted to slip the dough into the mixer and let the dough hook do the hard work for me. That said, I seldom feel I take as much pride in my dough as Nick does!

For enriched doughs such as brioche, however, I think that better results can be achieved by kneading in a machine. These doughs are often so soft and buttery that hand kneading encourages the fat to "oil" and the dough to become even less manageable. Such mixtures must have been very hard to work before the arrival of labor-saving gadgetry of the modern kitchen.

Gadgets are now available to produce freshly baked bread for you at any time and without any effort. You simply have to add the ingredients for your loaf to the unit, set the timer and leave the machine to it. It mixes, kneads, proofs, and bakes. It's convenient – but not much fun for dedicated bakers like us!

Before getting down to the nitty-gritty of bread making it would be useful to look at the ingredients in bread – the two most important being flour and yeast.

Different flours with different characteristics

No two flours react in the same way and, indeed, the same flour may have a different absorption rate in the summer and winter. It might sound like an almighty cop-out but all flour and liquid quantities given in this book really should be regarded as a guide only, although they are accurate as tested. For example, we have found that baking with organic flour, which is delightful to handle and much silkier than other bread flours, usually requires slightly less

Different flours for bread making.

liquid than regular flours. We are not talking dramatic differences here, merely the odd few drops, but it all makes a difference. This point further strengthens our argument in favor of mixing and kneading by hand, to really feel the dough.

Most breads are more successful when made with flour milled from hard wheat, such as bread flour. These contain more gluten (the protein that gives bread its structure) than soft, cake flours. Obviously bread flour is the ideal choice, but in the northern states most all-purpose flours are made from a blend of hard and soft wheat and are quite adequate for bread making. In the southern states, however, all-purpose flour is often made from soft wheat and is only suitable for quick breads. Breads baked with soft flour are much closer in texture as the dough does not develop so well. That said, a few recipes actually do call for soft flour when a closer texture is required in the final loaf or rolls.

We bake more brown bread than white but we do find that using all whole-wheat flour does not produce a very palatable bread – it is usually extremely heavy and often rather dry! We therefore use a mix of two-thirds whole-wheat flour to one third white bread flour, and find this to be an ideal combination for both texture and flavor.

Yeasts

There are two types of baker's yeast – compressed (fresh) and dried. In our opinion fresh yeast is unquestionably the best option – we feel it gives a superior flavor to the dough as well as giving a better

Compressed yeast, our favorite, with quick-rising yeast (right) and dried yeast (left).

rise and texture. It has a comparatively short shelf life – we never keep it for longer than 4 days – and it should be stored in the refrigerator, always tightly wrapped to prevent any air from getting to it and causing deterioration. We prefer to cover the yeast in plastic wrap rather than to keep it in a container which is also holding air.

Active dry yeasts

Active dry yeast has improved greatly over the past 10 years or so. Like compressed yeast it is first dissolved in liquid before mixing with the dry ingredients. Quick-rising yeast, in contrast, can be mixed directly into the dry ingredients and also reduces proofing times by about a third. When using any type of active dry yeast always read the package directions for specific mixing and proofing instructions and check the expiration date has not passed. Both these types of yeast sold in sealed packages or vacum-packed jars are a worthwhile store-cupboard ingredient for times of emergency.

Converting our recipes to active dry yeast

All the recipes in this book use compressed yeast, and we would recommend that you make every effort to find a supplier if you wish to bake regularly. A cake of compressed yeast weighs ⅗ ounce and as many of the recipes in this book use ½ to 1 ounce of yeast you will have to weigh your compressed yeast carefully. Should you wish to substitute active dry yeast 1 ounce of compressed yeast is equal to 1 tablespoon plus 2 teaspoons of active dry yeast. However if you want to use active dry yeast please note that it is not

suitable for flying ferment doughs. If you taste a bread baked with quick rising yeast, and then compare it with the same loaf made with compressed yeast and allowed to proof more slowly, we are confident that you will agree that the slower method is best! The longer you can leave the dough to proof, the more intense the flavor of the bread will be. This is why an overnight proofing produces such a wonderful flavor in morning rolls and brioche. The amount of yeast used in a dough will vary according to the richness of the mixture, so follow the recipes carefully.

Other raising agents

Not all breads are made with yeast – baking powder (breadsoda) is often used in quick breads, which are more like biscuit mixes, and bicarbonate of soda (baking soda) is used in some batter-like mixtures and in traditional Irish soda breads. Breads made with these raising agents are much quicker to prepare than yeasted varieties, and they definitely have their place in the modern cook's busy schedule.

Salt and sugar in bread

Bread made without salt is very bland but too much salt does the dough no good at all and will retard the action of the yeast. However, sugar has the opposite effect – it speeds up the action. When I was at college we were always told to put a little sugar in a dough but we seldom actually add it to our basic mixes now. It's rather like cooking onions – if you cook them slowly they develop a natural sweetness leading to a quite exceptional flavor. If you bake with compressed yeast and allow your dough to rise slowly, the natural sugars present will develop to flavor the dough.

Fats for freshness

Many commercially baked loaves contain very little fat and therefore go stale rather quickly. We always add oil, usually a good quality olive oil, to our basic breads as we find that it greatly improves their keeping qualities. I would not expect to toast our whole-wheat bread for breakfast until the fourth morning – if we have managed to resist it for that long!. Very plain breads certainly do not keep so well – a good example of this are French baguettes, which really have to be eaten on the day they are made.

Warm liquids for successful bread

The most common cause of failure when making bread is killing the yeast before it has had a chance to raise the dough. This happens when the bread is made with water or milk that is too hot. Yeast is killed at 140°F, so it should only be mixed with tepid liquid. The liquid is at the correct temperature when it feels neither hot nor cold to your little finger. Throughout this book we refer to lukewarm liquids for mixing – that means tepid.

Buttermilk used to be the residue left over at the end of butter-making but is now usually made from skim milk with a special culture added which begins to ferment during cooking, helping the rising process. It is used in place of sour milk and contributes a great depth of flavor to breads.

Basic techniques

To get a good result when making bread it is important to make a good dough. The easiest way to achieve this is to have a literally hands-on approach during mixing. Unless you actually touch the dough it is impossible to tell whether it is too dry or too wet and this will obviously greatly affect the final result of your labors.

A basic explanation here of the terms used in bread making will remove the need to duplicate procedures in every recipe. Many procedures are common to all bread making so it is as well to understand what is meant by each expression.

Mixing

Master bakers often mix their dough on the work surface, making a wall of flour and then filling it with the yeast liquid. The two are gradually worked together in a most impressive manner, but be warned! One slip of the fingers and the dam will be breached, resulting in yeast liquid all over the kitchen, down the units, in the drawers and over the floor – I know, it has happened to me! Mixing in a bowl is really much safer!

The most usual way to mix a dough is by placing all the dry ingredients in a bowl, making a well – a dip in the center to receive the liquid – and then stirring everything together. Once the dough starts to mix –

Start mixing your dough in a bowl (top) then turn it out onto the work surface to complete the mixing (center). This enables you to check that the dough is of the right consistency. The dough will be soft but not sticky when properly mixed (bottom).

to come together – we forsake the wooden spoon and work the dough with our hands. In this way you can tell if more flour or more liquid is required.

When a dough is too wet (above) and is sticking to the work surface during kneading, add a little extra flour on your hands until the dough no longer sticks. If a dough is too dry, add a little extra water on your hands in the same way.

Doughs that are sticky are usually too wet; doughs that feel heavy and very rigid are too dry.

Once the dough starts coming together we suggest turning it out onto the work surface to complete the mixing. More flour can then be added by sprinkling it onto the surface and working it gradually into the dough. It is often prudent to resist adding more flour until the kneading process is well under way – the dough will change in texture as it is kneaded and will become less sticky. We only add more flour at the end of mixing if the dough is completely un-workable and our hands and fingers stick together in the mass.

Adding more liquid

If a dough is too dry the temptation is to flatten it out, add some more liquid, fold it into the dough and then to work it through. The dough usually becomes sticky in places and remains dry in others, producing an uneven result. The best way that I have found to rectify this is to set the dough to rise for a short period, about 20-30 minutes, and then to knock it back and start the kneading properly. However, if more liquid is required I find it best to add it very gradually by wetting my hands in water and then working the dough. This distributes the liquid evenly and controls the amount that is added. You will also be immediately aware when the dough is at the correct consistency.

Kneading

Kneading is a process of stretching and working the dough to develop the gluten, the protein in the flour, to give the bread a structure. A well-kneaded dough is usually silky-smooth and shiny, with the ingredients all thoroughly blended and worked together. When the dough is properly kneaded it should be possible to stretch an "ear" of it away from the lump without it breaking off, showing the elastic nature of the dough.

I always used to think of kneading as basically giving the dough a hard time, a process that should be carried out to the most aggressive rock music to hand! Over the years, a lump of dough has represented the tax man and any number of other people who have ruffled my feathers! However, a better dough is produced if the kneading is more akin to a combination of stretching and punching, much of which is done with the heel of the hand. Stretch the dough away from you along the work surface, then bring it back, fold it over and stretch again.

Hand kneading is best

I have said before that Nick is a purist in his approach to kneading and he certainly always kneads by hand, producing a more open textured dough. We are both convinced that this hard manual work gives the best results – mixers just seem to work the dough in much the same way as my head-banging, hard rock

Stretch the dough away from you, using the heel of your hand (below) then press the dough back in to a ball (opposite top). The dough is properly kneaded when it is smooth and elastic – test the dough by teasing out the edge of the dough. It should stretch and not break (opposite bottom).

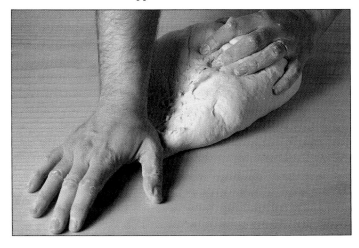

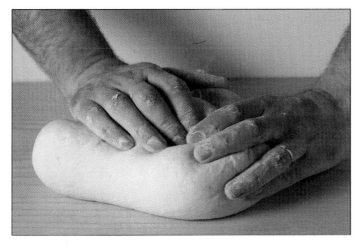

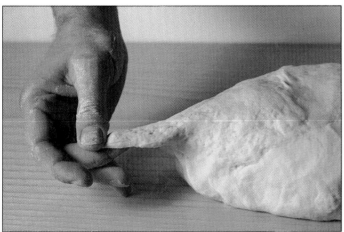

Dough should always be kept covered during this process, to prevent the surface from drying out and becoming crusty, which could lead to an uneven texture in the finished bread. Use a bowl with a lid, or cover the bowl with plastic wrap or a damp cloth. Oiled or floured plastic bags may also be used but choose a bag that is large enough to allow the dough to grow without it becoming stuck to the surface. We only use plastic bags in the initial stages of making croissants and pain au chocolat, when the quantity of dough is fairly small and relatively easy to handle.

Overnight proofing for flavor and convenience

One thing about bread making is that it is quite a long process, especially when you move on to enriched or sourdoughs, so it is important to plan your bread making properly. If you want freshly

approach. When I weaken and use the machine for this process I often use the general purpose beater and not the dough hook, as I feel this actually works the dough a little more thoroughly.

Some very sticky doughs may require kneading in the mixing bowl before being turned out onto the work surface. If a dough is intended to be sticky and is immediately kneaded on a floured surface the texture will change and the final result will not be as planned. Knead such doughs with a very lightly floured hand in the bowl, until smooth and workable – the stickiness will disappear as the dough is worked.

Proofing

Proofing is the process whereby a dough is set aside to rise and grow. It is usually done in a warm place, for example in a warm cupboard, but it is important to remember that yeast is killed at above 140°F, so the dough should not be allowed to become too warm – 100°F is the optimum temperature for proofing.

Place the kneaded dough in a bowl and cover with plastic wrap (top). The dough is proofed when the indentation remains after pressing with your finger (above).

baked bread for breakfast you don't want to have to get up at about 4am to achieve it!

An overnight proofing gives a very intense flavor to a fairly ordinary dough for morning rolls – you may have to rise at 6.30am to finish the shaping but this is a civilised hour compared to a professional baker's schedule! With brioche, the overnight proofing makes the very rich dough much easier to handle. Fresh croissants for breakfast would also be impossible without the overnight process.

We both hope that you will try the Three-day Sourdough recipe, but you must plan this properly – the final proofing times are very critical.

Punching Down or Knocking Back

These are both very descriptive terms for the short and gentle kneading that takes place in the middle of bread making. Once the dough has risen it must be shaped ready for baking. It is impossible to shape a dough that is stretchy and full of air so the dough must be re-kneaded to make it workable, by removing all the air from it. The risen dough is scraped out of its bowl onto a lightly floured work surface and is then lightly worked until it returns to its original size.

Shaping the dough

There are three main terms for the shaping and folding processes.

The mid-air fold is not really a fold at all, but a way of teasing out a dough to a circle. Hold the dough as you would the steering wheel of your car and rotate it quickly through your fingers, pressing it out into a larger, flatter shape. This technique is used in the

Mid-air fold – work the dough into a smooth round shape by pressing it with your thumbs and stretching it with your fingers.

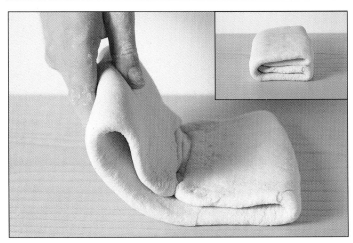

"Punch" the air out of the dough with your knuckles (top), then gently reshape the dough into a round (above).

Bookfold – fold both ends of the dough into the center (main picture above) then fold the dough in half again (insert).

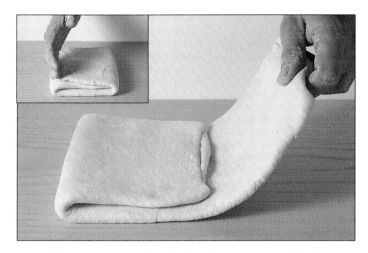

Gatefold – fold one third of the dough over the middle, then fold the remaining third over (main picture). Seal the edge of the dough lightly with the edge of your hand (insert).

most impressive of pizza houses where the chef is on show to the diners and a small lump of dough can quickly become a 10-inch pizza base. One advantage of this technique is that the dough is shaped without extra flour being added to it – too much can make the dough dry and heavy.

The bookfold is where a dough is rolled out to a rectangle and the sides are then folded over towards the center, meeting in the middle. The gatefold is similar but you mentally divide the dough into three. First one side is folded two thirds of the way

Shaping French sticks, baguettes, bread sticks etc.

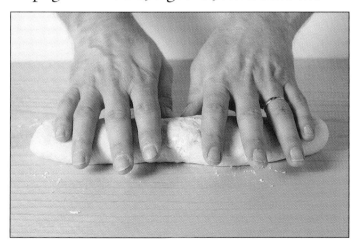

Roll out the dough pressing down firmly but evenly and moving your fingers along the whole length of the bread. We find using the bottom of your fingers and the back of your knuckles gives the best results. Have flour on the dough or on the work surface, not both or the dough will slip rather than roll.

across the dough, and then the remaining side is folded back across to give a little stack of three layers. Both these folds are used for flaky doughs such as croissants and Danish pastries, to achieve the layers.

Shaping croissants

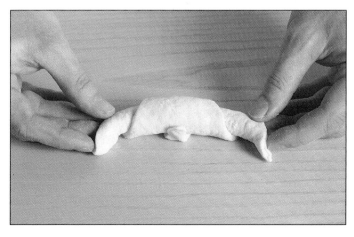

Stretch the corners of the dough (top) then stretch the tip (center). Roll up the croissant then fold the ends round into the traditional croissant shape (bottom).

Other techniques

Flying ferments

When I first met Nick he was making bread by a fermentation method which he continues to use for our everyday loaves. It is a good method for beginners as it is very "hands on" and you'll quickly get to learn the correct consistency of the dough.

Instead of starting with the flour and adding the liquid you work the other way around. Starting with the total quantity of liquid you add the yeast and some of the flour and leave that for 15 minutes or so to "sponge." This mixture is called a flying ferment. Extra flour is then added until the dough is the correct consistency for turning out onto the work surface and kneading. Such a method is not only good for beginners but is also ideal for partially-

sighted bread makers, who may find the weighing and measuring of ingredients quite difficult. The method is fully explained in the recipe for The Moon's Whole-wheat Loaf.

Sourdoughs

A lucky accident

It is generally accepted that cheese was first made when herdsmen discovered that left-over milk soured and turned into edible solids. A similar thing happened in the bread making world. It was found that a porridge of flour or grains and water would begin to ferment after two or three days and that, if extra flour was added, the fermentation could be used to raise a bread, giving a light texture and a more developed flavor to the final baked result. This was the start of the sourdough baking tradition, which is still popular in many countries, and especially among those who do not have ready access to yeast.

Sourdoughs – the pioneer's bread

I think of sourdoughs as pioneers' breads – they are often made in remote places where yeast is not available but everyone has plenty of time, and daily baking is as much a part of life as breathing and sleeping. One leaven will keep going for months but will eventually lose its freshness. It is then thrown away and the process begins all over again. However, even with easy access to fresh yeast and a wide variety of flours I actually prefer to make sourdough just occasionally, as a change from the now more traditional yeasted breads. Nick and I therefore make

Dissolve the yeast in warm liquid then add some flour (top). Stir to a creamy consistency (above). Cover and leave in a warm place until frothy then add the remaining flour (opposite top).

the Three-day Sourdough, as it is a self-contained recipe and no sponge is kept to start another batch. It is also less temperamental than some of the spongier recipes.

The leaven and the lump

The first step in making a sourdough is a starter, a pot of fermenting flour and water, which will raise the bread. The mixture should be left in a warm place for two or three days to allow the fermentation to begin – draughts and temperature fluctuations will slow the process down so it is often a good idea to wrap this type of mixture in a large, thick towel or blanket during all stages of preparation, to help to keep the mixture at a constant temperature.

The starter is then fed with more flour and water and left to form a sponge, which is the real leaven. Each time a traditional sourdough is mixed, a little is reserved to be refreshed to become the sponge for the next dough. The proofing time for sourdoughs is days rather than hours and the process really should not be hurried – the longer the proofing the more developed the flavor of the bread will be.

A combination of sourdough and yeast

A good halfway house is to make a sourdough which does not rely entirely on natural fermentation but also includes some yeast. In many ways this seems like cheating to us when we are in a purist frame of mind, but it does allow for a better rise and a less temperamental dough, while benefiting from the sourdough flavor. Such breads may be started from a potato or a flour mix. The Light Rye Sourdough is a good example.

Oven techniques

You are more likely to spoil a bread by baking it in an oven that is too cold than too hot. Brick ovens were fired up to very high temperatures and the baking was carried out in the residual heat. Traditional bakers, especially those using wood-fired ovens, still cook in this way. Breads and rolls are cooked first, when the oven is at its hottest, and then cakes and cookies are baked as the temperature drops. Breads are often called "morning goods" since this is generally when they are baked – remember

that a baker's day begins very early, when most sensible people are still asleep.

A good baker's tip to remember when baking French sticks is to place a roasting pan of water in the bottom of the oven during baking. This will create some steam and help to achieve a good texture. If your oven has an element in the oven floor, place the pan of water on a low shelf in the oven.

Cooking from cold

It is generally accepted that bread should be placed in a very hot oven for the best results. However for years we have baked our standard loaves from cold with excellent results and this has confounded many experts with whom we have discussed the matter! The method works well in fan ovens, and we have also cooked from cold in conventional electric ovens with success. Cooking times may be 5 minutes longer but we have found that the loaves have an excellent final rise.

I once demonstrated this technique on television and received a letter from a viewer who had tried to make bread for years without success. After watching my program she tried again, this time cooking from a cold start, with very satisfactory results. She was absolutely delighted! The Moon's Whole-wheat Loaf recipe is written for a cold start – by coincidence the recipe also uses a flying ferment but the two techniques do not necessarily go hand in hand; it's just the way we make our usual bread in a conventional oven.

Common problems

Holes in your dough

Occasionally, large holes develop in loaves during baking for no obvious reason. This does not necessarily mean your technique has failed. If you are sure that the dough has not been underkneaded (if kneaded by hand) or overkneaded (if kneaded by machine), then unfortunately you will just have to shrug your shoulders and take the baker's attitude. I have heard master bakers attribute holes in their dough to the weather and all sorts of other unlikely causes. Suffice it to say that you should just carry on as before, and hopefully the problem will clear itself.

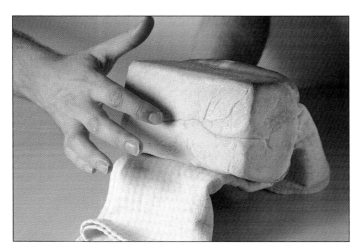

To check that bread is cooked, tap the base firmly – the bread should sound hollow.

Is it cooked yet?

Bread is cooked when the base of the loaf sounds hollow when tapped. Remove the bread from the pan and tap the base lightly with your knuckle. If the top crust is well browned but the loaf still doesn't really sound hollow, return the bread to the oven without the pan, just placing it on the wire shelf, and bake for a further 5 minutes

Unsatisfactory texture

If your loaf is too dry or rather crumbly it is usually because there was too much flour in the dough or the oven temperature was too high. If the loaf tastes dense and soggy either too much liquid was used or the dough has not been properly kneaded.

Inadequate rising

When a loaf does not rise very well or does not rise at all it is generally due to a problem with the yeast. Yeast is a living organism which is greatly affected by temperature and as a consequence it will be killed if mixed with a liquid that is too hot, or if it is left to rise in a place that is either too hot or too cold.

Cracked Crusts

Loaves sometimes develop a crack in the surface of the dough which causes the bread to rise unevenly in the oven. This simply means that the dough did not proof sufficiently after shaping and before it was put into the oven. The bread begins to cook before the final rising is over, and the action of the yeast forces the newly formed crust to split open. To combat this, make certain that a shaped dough does not more than half fill a baking pan, and that you allow it to rise to the top of the pan before placing the bread in the oven to cook. This is of great importance when cooking in a preheated oven. We find that breads baked from cold often have a final rising while the oven is heating up, but that it is even and seldom causes dramatic cracks.

Avoiding indigestion

No matter how tempting your bread smells when you take it from the oven, you should always let it cool for at least 20 minutes before eating it, otherwise it might cause indigestion. The exceptions to this rule are rolls and croissants which can be eaten after about 10 minutes – being smaller they cool down more quickly. Very hot bread is not easy to digest.

Complete culinary satisfaction

Bread making really is fun and so rewarding. This simple food can make the centerpiece of a meal and one of our favorite ways of relaxing at the weekend is to bake a fresh loaf and then to enjoy it with cheese, salami, salad and a bottle of wine. Simple pleasures are often best. We hope that you will find some new pleasures within these pages.

A white "split" loaf

This is a good standard bread; its preparation shows all the basic techniques of bread making.

You will need:
1 ounce compressed yeast
3¾ cups lukewarm water
12 cups bread or all-purpose flour
1 tablespoon salt
2 tablespoons oil
Flour for dusting

1   Crumble the yeast into 1¼ cups of the water and leave for 5 minutes.

2   Place the flour and salt together in a large mixing bowl, make a well in the center and add the oil.

3   Stir the yeast until dissolved then add this to the flour with most of the remaining 2½ cups of water. Mix together, adding the rest of the water if necessary.

4   Turn the dough out onto a lightly floured surface and finish mixing it together.

5   Knead the dough firmly for about 10 minutes, until it is smooth and elastic.

6   Return the dough to the bowl, cover and leave to proof in a warm place for about 1 hour, until doubled in bulk.

7   Turn the dough out onto the work surface and punch it down. Divide into two and shape into loaves, rolling the dough into shape.

8   Place the dough into two oiled 8½ x 4½ x 2½-inch loaf pans; cover and leave for about 30 minutes, until well risen and puffy.

9   Preheat the oven to 425°F while the loaves are rising.

10   Slash deeply along the length of each loaf with a serrated-edge knife or a sharp blade, then scatter a little extra flour over the loaves.

11   Bake in the preheated oven for about 45 minutes, until the bases sound hollow when tapped.

12   Remove the bread from the pans immediately and cool on a wire rack.

Step 1
Crumble the yeast into water.

Step 3
Stir the yeast until dissolved.

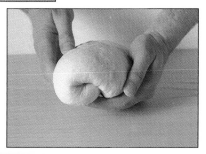

Step 7
Turn the dough out onto the work surface and punch it down.

Step 7
Divide into two and shape into loaves, rolling the dough into shape.

Step 8
Place the dough into two oiled loaf pans

Step 10
Slash deeply along the length of each loaf with a serrated-edge knife.

Possible finishes left to right: poppy seeds, beaten egg, flour for dusting, sesame seeds.

Chapter 1
Plain Breads

English Cottage Milk Loaf • Soft Brown Rolls • Baguettes

The Moons' Whole-wheat Bread • French Stick

Oatmeal Bread • Morning Rolls • French Country Bread

Light Rye Bread • Saffron Stick • Bread Sticks

Three-Day Sourdough Bread • Burger Buns • Pumpernickel

Pita Bread • Light Rye Sourdough • Ciabatta • Pretzels

Buttermilk Rye Bread • Bagels • Chapatties

Naan Bread • Wheat Flour Tortillas

ENGLISH COTTAGE MILK LOAF

Breads made with milk have a much softer crust than those made with water – this is ideal for cottage loaves as it makes them easier to slice. We sometimes add ground sunflower seeds to the flour for this bread.

MAKES 1 LARGE LOAF

½ ounce compressed yeast
Scant 2 cups lukewarm milk
6 cups bread flour or all-purpose flour
1 teaspoon salt
¼ cup butter
Beaten egg to glaze
Poppy seeds

1. Crumble the yeast into half the milk and leave for 3-4 minutes, then stir to completely dissolve the yeast.

2. Mix the flour and salt together then cut in the butter. Make a well in the center and pour in the yeast liquid. Mix to a soft but manageable dough, adding as much of the remaining milk as necessary.

3. Turn out onto a lightly floured surface and knead thoroughly until smooth and elastic. Return the dough to the bowl, cover and leave in a warm place for 45-60 minutes, until doubled in bulk.

4. Punch the dough down and divide into two, one piece being about double the size of the other.

5. Shape the larger piece of dough into a round loaf and place it on a floured baking sheet. Shape the small piece into a round and place it on top. Flour you index finger, or the handle of a wooden spoon and press it firmly through the center of the topknot, down to the baking sheet, to seal the two together. Cover loosely

Step 2 Add the yeast liquid to the flour and mix to a soft but manageable dough.

and leave in a warm place for about 30 minutes, until the loaf is well risen.

6. Brush the loaf with beaten egg and sprinkle some poppy seeds over the top of the loaf. Bake in a preheated 425°F oven for 30-35 minutes, until the loaf sounds hollow when tapped underneath. Transfer to a wire rack to cool.

Step 5 Press your index finger firmly through the two pieces of dough to seal them together.

Cook's Notes

Time
Preparation takes about 2 hours, cooking takes 30-35 minutes.

Variation
Make 3-4 slashes down the sides of the smaller round, then sprinkle some flour over the loaf before baking.

Cook's Tip
Make sure you seal the topknot on firmly.

SOFT BROWN ROLLS

These rolls have the same silky texture as the Morning Rolls, making them
the perfect soft rolls for those who prefer brown bread to white.

MAKES 18 ROLLS

Overnight dough
1 ounce compressed yeast
Scant 2 cups water
4 cups bread flour or all-purpose flour
½ ounce salt

Morning dough
1 ounce compressed yeast
⅔ cup lukewarm water
3½ cups whole-wheat flour
¼ cup butter
1 tablespoon sugar

Wheat germ for baking

1. To prepare the overnight dough, add the yeast to the water and stir until it has dissolved.

2. Add the yeast liquid to the flour and salt in a large mixing bowl, stirring them together. Do not knead at this stage. Cover and leave to proof overnight at room temperature.

3. In the morning add the morning dough ingredients to the overnight dough, dissolving the yeast in the warm water first. Mix in well, then turn out and knead on a

Step 3 Add the morning dough ingredients to the overnight dough.

lightly floured surface for about 10 minutes, or until smooth and elastic.

4. Divide the dough into 18 pieces of 3 ounces each. Shape the rolls by rolling them in circles under your palms, pressing down firmly. Gradually raise your hand while curling in your fingers to produce smooth rounds.

5. Place the rolls on floured baking sheets. Cover and leave to rise for about 30 minutes.

6. Scatter a little wheat germ over the rolls, pressing it very lightly onto the surface, then bake the rolls in a preheated 425°F oven for about 20 minutes. They should be lightly browned on top but still soft and not too crusty. Cool the rolls on a wire rack.

Cook's Notes

Time
Preparation takes 10 minutes plus overnight rising, then another 1 hour the next morning. Cooking takes about 20 minutes.

Variation
Finish the rolls with cracked wheat, poppy seeds or whole-wheat flour instead of wheat germ.

Cook's Tip
Add the butter in small pieces in Step 3 – it soon gets worked into the dough. You cannot cut butter into an overnight ferment.

BAGUETTES

Baguettes have a close but light texture and are softer
than French Sticks. The frequent brushing with water prevents the loaves
from burning during their long cooking time.

MAKES 2 LOAVES

1 ounce compressed yeast
⅔ cup lukewarm water
4 cups bread flour or all-purpose flour
1½ teaspoons salt

1. Crumble the yeast into the warm water and leave for 3-4 minutes, then stir until completely dissolved.

2. Mix the flour and salt together in a bowl and make a well in the center.

3. Add the yeast liquid and mix to a firm but manageable dough, then turn out onto a lightly floured surface and knead until smooth and elastic.

Step 5 Place the baguettes on floured baking sheets.

Step 6 Make diagonal slashes across the loaves before baking.

4. Return the dough to the bowl, cover and leave for about 1 hour in a warm place, until doubled in bulk.

5. Punch the dough down, divide it into two pieces and shape them into batons about 14 inches long (see introduction). Place the loaves on floured baking sheets, then cover and leave for another 20 minutes.

6. Brush the loaves with cold water, then make diagonal slashes across the top of each loaf.

7. Put the loaves in a preheated 400°F oven and, at the same time, place a roasting pan of cold water in the bottom of the oven. Bake for about 1 hour, brushing the loaves with cold water every 15 minutes. Cool on a wire rack.

Cook's Notes

Time
Preparation takes about 2 hours, cooking takes 1 hour.

Cook's Tip
All French breads are best eaten on the day that they are made.

Serving Idea
Slice the bread vertically in 4-inch chunks to make French-style filled rolls.

THE MOON'S WHOLE-WHEAT BREAD

This is our standard bread at home and we always bake it from a cold start, to give an extra rise to the loaves. We sometimes use spelt flour in place of the whole-wheat to give a distinctively sweet and nutty flavor.

MAKES 2 LARGE LOAVES

1 ounce compressed yeast
3¾ cups lukewarm water
7 cups whole-wheat flour
1 tablespoon salt
2 tablespoons olive oil
4 cups bread flour or all-purpose flour

1. Crumble the yeast into the warm water and stir until dissolved. Begin adding the whole-wheat flour until a creamy consistency is reached – this should take about half the flour. Cover and leave in a warm place to rise for 20 minutes.

2. Add the salt and olive oil, then work in the remaining

Step 1 Add enough whole-wheat flour to the yeast liquid to give a creamy consistency.

Step 2 Add the salt and olive oil.

flours to give a manageable dough.

3. Turn out onto a lightly floured work surface and knead for 10-15 minutes, until smooth and pliable. Return the dough to the bowl, cover and leave to rise for another 40 minutes.

4. Punch the dough down and divide it into two pieces. Shape into loaves and place them in two oiled 8½ x 4½ x 2½-inch bread pans. Leave to rise for about 20 minutes, loosely covered, until the dough is just above the rims of the pans.

5. Put the loaves in a **cold** oven, set the thermostat to 425°F and bake for 45 minutes. The loaves are cooked if they sound hollow when tapped underneath. Cool on a wire rack.

Cook's Notes

Time
Preparation takes about 2 hours, cooking takes about 45 minutes.

Cook's Tip
If the loaves are not quite done after 45 minutes, take them out of the pans, return them to the oven and bake for another 5 minutes.

Preparation
If cooking in a preheated oven, ensure that the loaves are well risen in the bread pans before baking.

FRENCH STICK

The dough for a French Stick is particularly hard and may seem
dry in comparison with others. It is best mixed in the evening and left to
rise overnight for cooking in the morning.

MAKES 3 OR 4 LOAVES

1 ounce compressed yeast
2 cups lukewarm water
8 cups bread flour or all-purpose flour
3½ teaspoons salt
1 beaten egg, for glazing

1. Crumble the yeast into ½ cup of the water and leave
for 5 minutes. Stir to completely dissolve the yeast.

2. Mix the flour and salt in a bowl and add the yeast
liquid and enough of the remaining water to mix to a
firm dough.

3. Knead the dough well on a lightly floured surface,
until it is smooth and the consistency of modeling clay.

4. Return the dough to the bowl, cover and leave for 12
hours at room temperature.

5. This amount of dough will make two loaves, each 24
inches long, but as most domestic ovens are not big
enough to accommodate loaves of this size, the dough
can be divided into three or four pieces and rolled out
into shorter batons (see introduction).

6. Place the shaped loaves on floured baking sheets
and leave to rise for another 2-3 hours. Cover the
loaves with damp cloths during this rising.

7. Brush the loaves with beaten egg then slash them
diagonally along the top. Place them in a preheated
500°F oven, then lower the heat immediately to 450°F
and bake for 20 minutes. Cool on a wire rack.

Step 7 Brush the
loaves with beaten
egg and slash them
diagonally before
baking.

Cook's Notes

Time
Preparation takes about 20
minutes plus overnight rising, then
another 2¼-3¼ hours the next day.
Cooking takes 20 minutes.

Cook's Tip
French sticks should have a
really stiff dough – modeling clay is
an excellent description of the correct
consistency. If the mixture is too wet
the bread will be doughy.

Cook's Tip
Make garlic bread by cutting
slits across the stick (being careful
not to cut right through), fill with garlic
butter and freeze.

OATMEAL BREAD

The addition of oatmeal gives a nutty taste and a coarse texture to this bread. The recipe is loosely based on a traditional Scottish loaf – oatmeal is used extensively in Scottish cookery.

MAKES 1 LARGE OR 2 SMALL LOAVES

¾ ounce compressed yeast
1 cup lukewarm water
1¾ cups whole-wheat flour
1 cup bread flour or all-purpose flour
¾ cup medium oatmeal
1 teaspoon salt
2 tablespoons oil
Oatmeal for dusting

1. Crumble the yeast into the warm water and leave for 3-4 minutes. Stir until the yeast is completely dissolved.

2. Mix the flours together with the oatmeal and salt in a bowl, making a well in the center. Add the oil and the yeast liquid, then mix to a firm but workable dough.

3. Turn onto a lightly floured surface and knead firmly until smooth – add a little extra flour if necessary as the dough should not be sticky.

4. Return the dough to the bowl, cover and leave in a warm place for about 1 hour, until doubled in bulk.

5. Punch the dough down gently, then shape and place in one 8½ x 4½ x 2½-inch bread pan, or two 7½ x 3½ x 2-inch pans. Cover and leave for about 30 minutes in a warm place, until it has risen to the top of the pan.

Step 2 Add the oatmeal to the flour in a bowl and mix together.

Step 6 Sprinkle a little extra oatmeal over the loaf before baking.

6. Sprinkle a little extra oatmeal over the loaf then bake in a preheated 450°F oven for about 30 minutes. Cool on a wire rack.

Cook's Notes

Time
Preparation takes about 2 hours, cooking takes about 30 minutes.

Variation
Add 1-2 tablespoons freshly chopped sage or parsley to the flours and oatmeal before mixing.

MORNING ROLLS

These are often called Scottish rolls and are silky smooth and creamy in texture.

MAKES 18 ROLLS

Overnight dough
1 ounce compressed yeast
Scant 2 cups water
4 cups bread flour or all-purpose flour
½ ounce salt

Morning dough
1 ounce compressed yeast
⅔ cup lukewarm water
4 cups bread flour or all-purpose flour
¼ cup butter, softened
1 tablespoon sugar

1. To prepare the overnight dough add the yeast to the water in a bowl, leave for 3-4 minutes then stir until it has all dissolved.

2. Mix the flour with the salt and add to the yeast liquid. Combine by stirring them together. Do not knead at this stage. Cover and leave to proof overnight at room temperature.

3. In the morning add the morning dough ingredients to the overnight dough, dissolving the yeast in the warm water first. Mix in well using your hands or a wooden spoon. Turn out and knead on a lightly floured surface to a smooth and pliable dough, about 10 minutes.

4. Divide the dough into 18 pieces of 3 ounces each. Shape the dough pieces into smooth round rolls by

Step 2 Add the flour and salt to the yeast liquid and stir.

rolling them under your palm in a circular motion, pressing down firmly. Gradually raise your hand while curling in your fingers to produce smooth rounds. Place them on floured baking sheets then cover and leave to rise about 30 minutes.

5. Bake the rolls in a preheated 425°F oven for about 20 minutes. They should be golden on top but still soft and not too crusty. Cool on a wire rack.

Step 3 Add the flour and the remaining morning dough ingredients to the overnight dough.

Cook's Notes

⏱ Time
Preparation takes 5 minutes plus overnight rising, then another 1 hour the next day. Cooking takes about 20 minutes.

Cook's Tip
Place the rolls quite close together on the baking sheets, so that they grow together, keeping the edges of the rolls soft during baking.

Preparation
Add the butter in small pieces in step 3 – it soon gets worked into the dough. You cannot cut butter into an overnight ferment.

FRENCH COUNTRY BREAD

This is a light rustic bread – the addition of just a little whole-wheat
flour gives it a slightly nutty texture.

MAKES 1 LARGE LOAF

1 ounce compressed yeast
1½ cups lukewarm water
4 cups bread flour or all-purpose flour
¾ cup whole-wheat flour
1 tablespoon salt

1. Crumble the yeast into the warm water and leave for
3-4 minutes, then stir to completely dissolve the yeast.

2. Mix the flours and salt together in a large bowl, make
a well in the center then add the yeast liquid and mix to
a firm but manageable dough.

3. Turn out onto a floured surface and knead for about 10
minutes, until the dough is smooth and elastic in texture.

Step 6 Surround the
loaf with a clean
folded cloth, so that it
holds its shape and
rises upwards.

Step 7 Score the
bread deeply three
times before baking.

4. Return the dough to the bowl, cover and leave in a
warm place for about 1 hour, or until doubled in bulk.

5. Punch the dough down and reshape it, then return it
to the bowl, cover and leave it for another 30 minutes in
a warm place.

6. Lightly flour a baking sheet. Knead the dough again
and shape it into a round loaf. Place it on the baking
sheet, surround it with a clean folded cloth, so that it
holds its shape and rises upwards. Cover and proof
again for 45 minutes or until doubled in bulk. This is the
third rising.

7. Score the bread deeply three times, then bake in a
preheated 475°F oven for 30-35 minutes. Cool on a
wire rack.

Cook's Notes

🕐 **Time**
Preparation takes about 3 hours,
cooking takes 30-35 minutes.

🎩 **Cook's Tip**
The extra rising gives this bread
its typically French light and airy
texture.

LIGHT RYE BREAD

Rye bread makes a very pleasant change from the traditional wheat loaves, but we like to make the bread with only half rye flour, finding that it gives a lighter texture.

MAKES 1 LARGE LOAF

½ ounce compressed yeast
Scant 2 cups mixed lukewarm milk and water
3 cups rye flour
3 cups bread flour or all-purpose flour
1 teaspoon salt
3 tablespoons olive oil
Extra flour

1. Crumble the yeast into about ⅔ cup of the warm liquid and leave it for 3-4 minutes. Stir to dissolve the yeast completely.

2. Mix the flours and salt together in a large bowl and make a well in the center. Add the oil, the yeast liquid and as much of the remaining liquid as necessary to make a soft, manageable dough.

3. Turn it out onto a floured surface and knead thoroughly until smooth and elastic. Return the dough to the bowl, cover and leave in a warm place for about 1 hour, until almost doubled in bulk.

4. Punch the dough down and shape into an oval loaf. Place on a floured baking sheet, cover and leave in a warm place for another 30 minutes.

5. Scatter a little extra flour over the loaf then bake it in a preheated 425°F oven for 35-40 minutes. Cool on a wire rack.

Step 2 Mix together the flours and salt.

Step 2 Add the yeast liquid and mix.

Cook's Notes

Time
Preparation takes about 2 hours, cooking takes 35-40 minutes.

Cook's Tip
Although this is a rye dough, the rye flour is mixed with wheat flour, which still gives the loaves a good rise.

SAFFRON STICK

Saffron has such an unmistakable scent that it adds a touch of luxury
to anything from the humble loaf to the richest of rice dishes.

MAKES 1 LARGE LOAF

½ ounce compressed yeast
1 cup lukewarm water
4 cups bread flour or all-purpose flour
1 teaspoon salt
Large pinch of powdered saffron
3 tablespoons olive oil

1. Crumble the yeast into the warm water and leave for 5 minutes.

2. Mix the flour and salt together in a bowl. Add the saffron to the yeast liquid and whisk well until dissolved.

3. Add the yeast liquid to the flour with the olive oil and mix to a stiff, manageable dough, adding a little more water if necessary. Turn out onto a floured surface and knead until smooth and elastic.

4. Return the dough to the bowl, cover and leave in a warm place for about 1 hour, until doubled in bulk.

5. Knead the dough again then roll it out with your hands to form a stick about 15-18 inches long. Place on a floured baking sheet, cover and leave for another 20-30 minutes, until risen.

Step 2 Add the saffron to the yeast liquid and whisk well until dissolved.

Step 5 Place the saffron stick on a floured baking sheet.

6. Slash the bread about 6 times with a serrated knife or a sharp blade, then scatter the loaf with a little flour. Bake in a preheated 450°F oven for 25 minutes. Cool on a wire rack before serving warm.

Cook's Notes

Time
Preparation takes about 2 hours, cooking takes 25 minutes.

Variation
Add 2 ounces sesame seeds to the dough mix for a crunchy textured bread.

Serving Idea
Serve with cheese, salami or dishes with lots of juices to mop up, such as mussels.

BREAD STICKS

Bread sticks (*Grissini*) are a staple part of Italian meals – especially in restaurants, where they are often served as a pre-dinner nibble.

MAKES 24

½ ounce compressed yeast
Scant 1 cup mixed lukewarm milk and water
3 cups bread flour or all-purpose flour
1 teaspoon salt

1. Crumble the yeast into the warm liquid and leave for 3-4 minutes, then stir to completely dissolve the yeast.

2. Mix the flour and salt together in a bowl then add the yeast liquid and mix to a stiff but manageable dough.

Step 3 Knead the stiff dough until smooth and elastic.

Step 4 Divide the dough into pieces then roll out into long thin sticks.

3. Turn out onto a lightly floured surface and knead thoroughly until smooth and elastic. Return the dough to the bowl and leave covered in a warm place for 1-1½ hours, until doubled in bulk.

4. Punch down the dough and divide it into 24 pieces. Roll each piece out into a long, thin stick. Place on floured baking sheets, cover and leave to rise for another 20 minutes until slightly puffed.

5. Bake the bread sticks in a preheated 400°F oven for 15-20 minutes, until evenly browned and crisp. Cool on a wire rack.

Cook's Notes

Time
Preparation takes 2-2½ hours, cooking takes 15-20 minutes.

Variation
Scatter sesame seeds or coarse salt over the sticks before baking.

Cook's Tip
The bread sticks are cooked when they are crisp and snap easily.

THREE-DAY SOURDOUGH BREAD

As the name suggests this bread has a unique sour taste, due to
the lengthy natural fermentation of the flour.

MAKES 3 LOAVES

Day 1
4 cups whole-wheat flour
1 cup lukewarm water

Day 2
Scant 1 cup whole-wheat flour
3 cups bread flour or all-purpose flour
1 teaspoon salt
1 cup lukewarm water

Day 3
Scant 1 cup whole-wheat flour
3 cups bread flour or all-purpose flour
1¼ cups lukewarm water

1. Day 1; mix the flour and water together to form a firm dough. Leave covered at room temperature for 24 hours, but don't expect the dough to alter dramatically – it will probably still look the same.

2. Day 2; add the fresh ingredients to the dough to form a new firm dough. Work the dough together with your hands – this is quite a task! Leave covered in the bowl at room temperature for another 24 hours.

Step 2 Work the fresh ingredients into the dough with your hands.

Step 3 The dough rises significantly after the third rising.

Step 4 Score the loaves before baking.

3. Day 3; add the new ingredients to the dough, then turn onto a floured surface and knead until smooth. Leave covered in the bowl for 20 hours.

4. Day 4; punch the dough down and divide into three. Shape the loaves and place on floured baking trays or in bread pans. Leave to rise for at least 4 hours. Score the tops of the loaves with a sharp knife or blade.

5. Bake the loaves in a preheated 450°F oven for about 25 minutes, until they sound hollow when tapped underneath. Cool on a wire rack.

Cook's Notes

Time
Preparation takes 3 days, cooking (day 4) takes 25 minutes.

Cook's Tip
Don't give up at the end of the first day if nothing has happened to the dough – this is normal.

Watchpoint
Plan this bread carefully, to ensure you don't have to get up in the middle of the night for the last rising and shaping session!

BURGER BUNS

As well as being the perfect shape for serving with hamburgers these also make ideal lunch-box rolls as they are quite large and will hold a good deal of filling. They have a soft texture and are much easier to eat than crusty rolls.

MAKES 8

⅔ cup lukewarm milk
⅔ cup lukewarm water
½ ounce compressed yeast
4 cups bread flour or all-purpose flour
1 teaspoon salt
¼ cup lard or shortening

1. Mix the milk and water together and ensure that they are only just warm. Crumble the yeast into the liquid, leave for 2-3 minutes, then stir until dissolved.

2. Mix the flour and salt together in a large bowl then cut in the lard or shortening. Make a well in the middle and pour in the yeast liquid.

3. Mix to a soft but manageable dough, then turn onto a floured surface and knead for about 5 minutes, until the dough is smooth and elastic.

4. Place in a clean bowl, cover and leave at room temperature to rise for 1½ hours, until doubled in bulk.

5. Flour two baking sheets. Punch the dough down and divide it into 8 pieces. Shape each into a round and roll out until ½-inch thick. Place on the baking sheets, cover and leave to rise for 40 minutes.

Step 2 Make a well in the flour and pour in the yeast liquid.

6. Sprinkle the tops of the buns with some flour then bake in a preheated 400°F oven for 15-20 minutes, until pale golden in color. Cool on a wire rack.

Step 5 Roll out the buns then place them on the floured baking sheets.

Cook's Notes

Time
Preparation takes about 2¾ hours, cooking takes 15-20 minutes.

Variation
Use half whole-wheat and half white flour to make brown burger buns.

PUMPERNICKEL

This is the traditional dark rye bread of Germany, slightly acidic in flavor and delicious with sliced cheese and cold smoked meats.

MAKES 2 SMALL LOAVES

6 cups rye flour
1 tablespoon salt
¼ cup butter
2 tablespoons molasses
1¼ cups milk
¾ ounce compressed yeast
⅔ cup lukewarm water
1 tablespoon caraway seeds

1. Mix the rye flour and salt together in a bowl, then cut in the butter and make a well in the center.

2. Put the molasses and milk in a saucepan and heat gently until the molasses has dissolved. The milk should be no more than lukewarm.

3. Crumble the yeast into the warm water and leave it for 2-3 minutes, then stir to ensure that the yeast has dissolved. Add it to the flour with the milk, then mix to a sticky dough.

4. Turn onto a floured surface and knead the dough for about 10 minutes, working in a little more flour if necessary, until the dough is firm and no longer sticky.

5. Place the dough in a bowl, cover and leave in a warm place for 1-1½ hours, or until doubled in bulk.

6. Punch the dough down and knead it again lightly. Divide into two and shape the pieces into ovals, placing them on a floured baking sheet or shape them to fit two 7½ x 3½ x 2-inch bread pans.

Step 3 Add the molasses and milk to the flour with the yeast liquid.

Step 8 Lightly press the caraway seeds into the top of the loaves.

7. Cover the loaves and leave them to rise again until they have reached the top of the pans.

8. Lightly press the caraway seeds into the top of the loaves then bake them in a preheated 400°F oven for about 45 minutes. They should be dark brown on top and sound hollow when tapped underneath. Cool the loaves on a wire rack.

Cook's Notes

⏱ Time
Preparation takes 2¼-2¾ hours, cooking takes 45 minutes.

👨‍🍳 Cook's Tip
Be careful not to overheat the molasses and milk – it is very easy to kill the yeast if it becomes too hot.

PITA BREAD

These are the best known of all the flat breads. They are eaten throughout the Mediterranean with dips and barbecued meats.

MAKES 18 SMALL BREADS

½ ounce compressed yeast
1¼ cups lukewarm water
4 cups all-purpose flour
½ teaspoon salt

1. Crumble the yeast into half the water and stir until completely dissolved. Leave in a warm place, loosely covered, until the yeast bubbles – about 20 minutes.

2. Mix the flour and salt in a bowl and gradually add the yeast mixture. Stir with a wooden spoon while adding the rest of the water to form a stiff dough.

3. Knead the dough until it is smooth and elastic. Divide the dough into 18 pieces, cover and leave in a warm place for 30 minutes.

4. Roll out each piece of dough on a floured board to form a thin round. Sprinkle lightly with more flour, cover and leave for 1 hour.

5. Flatten the rounds and roll out again, then cover and leave for another 30 minutes.

6. Bake the pita breads in batches on a floured baking sheet at the top of a preheated 500°F oven for about 10 minutes; they will puff up but will flatten immediately when removed from the oven.

Step 3 Divide the dough into 18 pieces then leave them covered.

Step 4 Roll out to form thin rounds.

Cook's Notes

Time
Preparation takes about 3 hours, cooking takes 10 minutes per batch.

Cook's Tip
Do not allow the pitas to brown too much during baking – they should be only slightly browned.

Variation
Use the dough to make just 12 breads if you prefer them slightly thicker.

Serving Idea
Split the pita breads open, it may be necessary to warm them first, to reveal the "pocket." Stuff with salads and cheese or meat for a filling sandwich.

LIGHT RYE SOURDOUGH

The speed of a yeast dough is combined with a quick sourdough starter to make a really well-flavored loaf. The sourdough starter is best prepared overnight.

MAKES 2 SMALL LOAVES

½ ounce compressed yeast
Scant 2 cups milk
3 cups rye flour
3 cups bread flour or all-purpose flour
1 tablespoon salt

1. Crumble the yeast into a large bowl. Heat the milk until just lukewarm, add a little to the bowl and cream the yeast.

2. Add the remaining milk to the yeast along with 2 cups of the rye flour and mix to a thick paste. Cover the bowl and leave it in a warm place for 10-14 hours, or until the mixture is slightly frothy and smells sour – this

Step 3 Stir the remaining flours into the overnight ferment.

Step 5 Shape into 2 loaves and place on floured baking sheets.

is best done overnight.

3. The next morning mix in the remaining flours and the salt to form a firm but manageable dough. Knead the dough on a lightly floured surface until firm but elastic.

4. Place in a bowl, cover and leave in a warm place for about 1 hour, until doubled in bulk.

5. Punch the dough down and knead it lightly, then shape into two loaves. Place on floured baking sheets or in oiled bread pans and leave covered for another 30 minutes, or until well risen.

6. Bake the loaves in a preheated 425°F oven for 15 minutes then reduce the temperature to 375°F for another 20 minutes, until cooked. Cool on a wire rack.

Cook's Notes

Time
Preparation takes 10 minutes plus overnight rising, then another 2 hours the next day. Cooking takes about 35 minutes.

Variation
Add 1-2 teaspoons of caraway seeds to the overnight dough along with the remaining flour and salt.

Serving Idea
This bread is excellent served with pickled fish.

CIABATTA

Ciabatta is not the easiest of breads to make at home but the flavor is delicious. It is made with a sourdough-type starter – the secret of the true Italian flavor.

MAKES 4 LOAVES

Starter
¼ ounce compressed yeast
1 cup plus 2 tablespoons warm water
3 cups all-purpose flour

Dough
¼ ounce compressed yeast
5 tablespoons warm milk
1 cup plus 2 tablespoons warm water
1 tablespoon fruity olive oil
4¼ cups all-purpose flour
1 tablespoon salt

1. For the starter, add the yeast to the water, leave 3-4 minutes then stir until dissolved. Add the flour and mix well. Cover and leave at room temperature to stand for 12 hours.

2. For the dough, crumble the yeast into the milk in the bowl of an electric mixer. Stand for 3-4 minutes, then stir until dissolved. Add the water, oil and starter and mix with the beater until well blended.

3. Add the flour and salt and mix for 2-3 minutes. Change to the dough hook and knead for 2 minutes at a low speed, then 2 minutes at a medium speed.

4. Turn onto a lightly floured surface and knead lightly – add just enough flour to make it manageable. Return the dough to the bowl, cover and leave in a warm place for 1 hour, until doubled in bulk and full of bubbles.

5. Flour 4 pieces of baking parchment. Turn the dough out onto a well floured surface – do not punch it down, but divide it into four pieces. Roll into loaf shapes then press them flat, pulling them into rough rectangles of about 10 x 4 inches.

6. Place each loaf on a piece of parchment, smoothest side downwards, then dimple them firmly with your fingers. Cover and leave for 1½ hours. The loaves will become puffy but will not really rise very much.

7. Place 2 baking sheets in a preheated 425°F oven for 30 minutes to preheat. Turn the loaves over gently onto the hot baking sheets – be careful not to knock the air out. Remove the parchment and bake for 20-25 minutes until pale brown. Spray the loaves with a fine water mister three times during the first 10 minutes of baking. Cool briefly on wire racks and eat warm.

Step 6 Dimple the dough firmly with your fingers – this prevents the loaves from rising too much.

Step 7 Carefully remove the parchment from the loaves.

Cook's Notes

Time
Preparation takes 5 minutes plus overnight rising, then 3 hours the next day. Cooking takes 20-25 minutes.

Cook's Tip
Spraying the loaves with a water mister stops the loaves browning too much.

Preparation
This is a very soft dough, do not be tempted to add extra flour when first kneading it on the work surface.

PRETZELS

The secret of good pretzels is to roll the dough out thinly, so that the finished bread is not too chewy. The shaping is easily mastered.

MAKES 16

½ ounce compressed yeast
Pinch of sugar
⅔ cup lukewarm water
4 cup bread flour or all-purpose flour
1 teaspoon salt
⅔ cup milk
1½ tablespoons butter
1 large egg, beaten
Coarse salt

1. Crumble the yeast with the sugar into the water, leave for 3-4 minutes then stir to completely dissolve the yeast.

2. Mix the flour and salt in a bowl and make a well in the center. Pour in the yeast liquid and mix a little of the flour into the liquid. Cover the bowl and leave in a warm place for 10 minutes.

3. Warm the milk and butter in a saucepan until the butter is just melted and the liquid just lukewarm. Pour it into the flour and knead the mixture in the bowl (it will be too sticky to knead on a work surface) until it no longer sticks to the sides.

4. Cover again and leave to rise in a warm place for 1 hour or until doubled in bulk. Punch the dough down and knead on a floured surface for 10 minutes.

5. Divide the dough into 16 pieces and roll them out into pencil shapes about 14 inches long. Curve the ends to make a horseshoe, keeping the open end

Step 3 Knead the mixture in the bowl until it no longer sticks to the sides.

towards you, cross the ends and fold up onto the curve of the horseshoe, pressing together lightly. Place on a floured baking sheet, cover and leave for 10 minutes.

6. Brush the pretzels with the beaten egg and sprinkle with coarse salt. Place them in a preheated 450°F oven and immediately lower the temperature to 400°F. Bake the pretzels for 20 minutes or until they are golden brown. Cool on a wire rack.

Step 5 Cross the ends of the dough and fold back onto the curve of the horseshoe, pressing together lightly.

Cook's Notes

Time
Preparation takes about 2 hours, cooking takes about 20 minutes.

Cook's Tip
Some people poach pretzels for a few seconds before baking them – we have found it of no advantage.

Variation
Sprinkle with sesame seeds or poppy seeds instead of coarse salt.

BUTTERMILK RYE BREAD

I always think of this as a mid-European bread – the recipe is not authentic but it reminds me of breads eaten in Poland.

MAKES 2 ROUND LOAVES

½ ounce compressed yeast
⅔ cup lukewarm milk
3 cups rye flour
2⅔ cups whole-wheat flour
1 teaspoon salt
1 teaspoon grated nutmeg
3 tablespoons olive oil
1¼ cups buttermilk
Milk, rye flour and poppy seeds

1. Crumble the yeast into the milk and leave for 4-5 minutes before stirring to dissolve the yeast.

2. Mix all the dry ingredients together in a large bowl and make a well in the center. Pour in the oil, buttermilk and yeast liquid and mix well to form a soft but manageable dough.

Step 2 Mix all the dry ingredients together in a large bowl.

3. Turn out onto a lightly floured surface and knead thoroughly until smooth and elastic.

4. Return the dough to the bowl, cover and leave for

Step 5 Roll each piece of dough into a round.

Step 6 Scatter the scored dough with poppy seeds and the flour.

about 1 hour in a warm place, until almost doubled in bulk.

5. Punch the dough down, divide it into two then shape and roll each piece into a round about 8 inches in diameter. Place on baking sheets then cover and leave to rise for another 30-45 minutes, until puffy.

6. Brush the loaves with milk, then score each one into 8 portions. Scatter with rye flour and poppy seeds. Bake in a preheated 425°F oven for 30-40 minutes. Transfer to a wire rack to cool.

Cook's Notes

⏱ Time
Preparation takes about 2 hours, cooking takes 30-40 minutes.

🧑‍🍳 Cook's Tip
Remember that rye breads do not rise as much as other doughs, so don't expect too much.

BAGELS

Bagels are popular in Europe as well as America and make delicious rolls – we like them filled with cream cheese and smoked salmon.

MAKES 20

¼ cup butter
1 cup water
½ ounce compressed yeast
4 cups all-purpose flour
1 teaspoon salt
2 tablespoons superfine sugar

1. Place the butter and water in a saucepan and heat gently until the butter has melted – the mixture should be no more than lukewarm. Crumble the yeast into the liquid and leave for 3-4 minutes, then stir until the yeast is completely dissolved.

2. Place the flour, salt and sugar in a bowl and make a well in the center. Add the yeast liquid and mix to a dough. Turn out onto a floured board and knead until the dough is smooth and elastic, about 10 minutes. Place the dough in a bowl, cover and leave in a warm

Step 3 Roll the dough pieces out into short strips.

Step 3 Shape the dough into a ring, pinching the ends firmly together.

place for about 1½-2 hours or until doubled in bulk.

3. Punch the dough down, then divide it into 20 balls of equal size. Roll each ball out into a strip about 5 inches long and shape the strip into a ring, pinching the ends very firmly together so they do not come apart during cooking. Cover the bagels on a floured board. Leave them in a warm place for 45 minutes to rise.

4. Bring a large, shallow pan of water to a boil. Reduce the heat and when the water is simmering gently, drop a ring into it. As soon as it rises to the top, remove it with a slotted spoon. Drain on absorbent paper towels and repeat with the rest of the bagels.

5. Flour two baking sheets. Transfer the rings to the baking sheets and bake in a preheated 400°F oven for about 30 minutes until crisp and golden brown. Cool on wire racks.

Cook's Notes

Time
Preparation takes 3-3½ hours, cooking takes about 30 minutes.

Cook's Tip
Do not poach the bagels for too long or they will become difficult to handle and stick to the paper towel.

Variation
Top the bagels with poppy seeds, or toasted sesame seeds before baking.

CHAPATTIES

These breads, cooked on a griddle or a skillet, are one of the
easiest Indian breads to make.

MAKES 14

1 tablespoon butter
3 cups fine graham flour
½ teaspoon salt
¾-1¼ cups lukewarm water
1 tablespoon extra flour in a shallow bowl or plate

1. Cut the butter into the flour and salt then add enough of the warm water to form a soft dough.

2. Turn out onto a lightly floured surface and knead until smooth and elastic. Place the dough in a bowl, cover and leave for 30 minutes.

3. Divide the dough into 14 walnut-sized pieces. Roll each piece into a ball then flatten the balls and dip each one into the dry flour.

4. Roll each piece of dough out into a circle about 6 inches in diameter.

5. Heat an iron griddle or a skillet until evenly hot. Be careful not to overheat it as this will cause the chapatties to stick and burn. Cook the chapatties for 30 seconds on each side, until brown spots appear.

Step 3 Flatten the chapatties before dipping them in flour.

6. Keep the chapatties warm in a piece of foil lined with absorbent paper towel until they are all cooked.

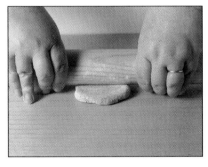

Step 4 Roll out the dough into thin circles.

Cook's Notes

Time
Preparation takes about 45 minutes, cooking takes about 15 minutes.

Cook's Tip
Hold your hand about 6 inches above the griddle – if your hand feels evenly warm the griddle is at the correct temperature for cooking.

Preparation
The exact quantity of water needed to make the dough depends on the texture and type of flour.

NAAN BREAD

These breads from the Indian subcontinent are traditionally cooked in a clay oven, a tandoor, but they can be cooked successfully in a very hot conventional oven.

MAKES 8

4 cups all-purpose flour
1 teaspoon salt
1 teaspoon sugar
⅓ cup milk
1 ounce compressed yeast
¼ cup butter
⅔ cup plain yogurt
1 large egg, beaten
2 tablespoons sesame seeds or poppy seeds

1. Place the flour, salt and sugar in a large bowl and mix together well.

2. Heat the milk until it is lukewarm, crumble in the yeast and leave for 3-4 minutes then stir until the yeast is completely dissolved. Melt the butter and cool until it is just lukewarm.

3. Add the yeast liquid, all but 1 tablespoon of the yogurt, the egg and melted butter to the flour. Mix to a soft dough then turn out onto a floured surface and knead until soft and elastic.

4. Place the dough in a clean bowl, cover and leave in a warm place for about 1 hour, until doubled in bulk.

5. Divide the dough into 8 balls, kneading them lightly then cover and leave for 10-15 minutes.

6. Place two ungreased baking sheets in a preheated 450°F oven for about 10 minutes to heat through. Remove the hot baking sheets from the oven and flour

Step 3 Add all but 1 tbsp of yogurt to the flour, egg, yeast liquid and butter.

them lightly.

7. Shape the balls by a mixture of mid-air folds (see introduction) and stretching or rolling into teardrop shapes about 6-7 inches long. Place on the baking sheets and brush with the reserved yogurt, then sprinkle with the sesame seeds or poppy seeds.

8. Bake one sheet at a time on the top shelf of the oven for about 10 minutes, or until puffed and browned.

Step 7 Shape the naan by rolling or mid-air folds into tear-drop shapes.

Cook's Notes

Time
Preparation takes 1¾-2 hours, cooking takes about 10 minutes.

Variation
Mix crushed garlic and freshly chopped coriander into the yogurt before glazing the naan breads.

WHEAT FLOUR TORTILLAS

These Mexican unleavened flat breads or pancakes made with wheat flour are easier to prepare than the corn ones. They may be filled and baked or fried.

MAKES 12

4 cups all-purpose flour
1 tablespoon salt
Scant ⅓ cup lard or shortening
1¼ cups hot water

1. Mix the flour and salt together in a bowl then cut in the lard or shortening until the mixture resembles bread crumbs. Gradually add the water to form a soft, pliable dough.

2. Knead the dough on a well-floured surface until smooth and no longer sticky. Divide the dough into 12

Step 1 Gradually add the water to form a soft, pliable dough.

Step 3 Cut into neat rounds using a plate as a guide.

pieces, keeping the dough that is not being worked covered to prevent it from drying out.

3. Knead each piece into a ball, then roll out each piece into a very thin circle, using a floured rolling pin. Cut into neat rounds using a 10-inch plate as a guide.

4. Stack the tortillas as you make them, flouring each one well to prevent them from sticking together. Cover with a clean cloth.

5. Heat a heavy-based griddle or skillet until evenly hot, and carefully add a tortilla. Cook for about 10 seconds per side. Stack and keep covered until all are cooked. Use according to your chosen recipe.

Cook's Notes

Time
Preparation takes 20-25 minutes, cooking takes about 5 minutes.

Cook's Tip
Do not overcook tortillas, they must be pliable or they will crack when rolled around a filling. They should still be pliable after the above cooking period.

Chapter 2

Savory Breads

Beer and Onion Bread • Tomato Focaccia

Pumpkin and Cheese Bread • Zucchini Bread

Poppy Seed and Anchovy Focaccia • Walnut Bread

Cheesy Malted Grain Rolls • Pesto Stick • Bacon and Cheese Bread

Sausage Brioche • Roman Focaccia • Spinach and Olive Oil Bread

Olive Bread • Mushroom Brioche • Basil and Goat's Cheese Focaccia

Sage and Orange Bread • Pizza Dough

BEER AND ONION BREAD

We very seldom use soup mixes in our cooking but a package of onion soup makes the perfect flavoring for this savory loaf.

MAKES 2 LOAVES

1¼ cups dark beer
¾ ounce compressed yeast
1¼ cups lukewarm water
4 cups bread flour or all-purpose flour.
3½ cups whole-wheat flour
1 teaspoon salt
1 ounce package onion soup mix
3 tablespoons oil
Onion rings for garnish

1. Pour the beer out and leave it to stand so that it becomes slightly flat.

2. Crumble the yeast into the warm water and leave for 3-4 minutes, then stir to completely dissolve the yeast.

3. Mix together the flours, salt and soup mix in a bowl and make a well in the center. Add the oil, yeast liquid and beer and mix to a manageable dough.

4. Turn onto a lightly floured surface and knead thoroughly until smooth and elastic. Return the dough to the bowl, cover and leave in a warm place for 45 minutes, or until doubled in bulk.

5. Punch the dough down and divide it into 2 pieces. Shape into round loaves and place in two oiled bread crocks or on floured baking sheets. Cover and leave for 30 minutes until well risen.

Step 3 Mix together the flours, salt and soup mix.

6. Soak some finely sliced onion rings in cold water for 15 minutes, then drain and dry them.

7. Press the onion rings lightly into the top of the dough then bake the loaves in a preheated 425°F oven for 30 minutes. Cool on wire racks.

Step 5 Place the dough in oiled bread crocks or on floured baking sheets.

Cook's Notes

Time
Preparation takes about 2 hours and cooking takes 30 minutes.

Cook's Tip
Bread crocks make attractive loaves and are well suited to savory breads such as this. You may need to bake the loaves for another 5 minutes out of the crock at the end of the cooking time to finish them off.

TOMATO FOCACCIA

This Italian bread is flavored with sun-dried tomatoes and fresh basil – we think it is the best tomato bread we have tasted!

MAKES 1 LOAF

8 halves sun-dried tomatoes in oil
1 ounce compressed yeast
½ cup lukewarm water
4 cups bread flour or all-purpose flour
1 teaspoon salt
1 teaspoon superfine sugar
4 large fresh basil leaves, finely chopped
¼ cup olive oil
1 tablespoon sun-dried tomato oil
½ cup passata
Coarse sea salt

1. Soak the sun-dried tomato halves in boiling water for 10 minutes, then rinse them in cold water and pull off the peels, or scrape off the flesh with a teaspoon. Chop the flesh finely.

2. Crumble the yeast into the warm water and leave for 3-4 minutes then stir to completely dissolve the yeast.

3. Mix together the flour, salt, sugar, chopped basil and tomatoes and make a well in the center. Add 3 table-spoons of the olive oil, the tomato oil, passata and the yeast liquid and and mix well to form a soft but manageable dough.

4. Turn out onto a floured surface and knead thoroughly until smooth and elastic. Return the dough to the bowl, cover and leave in a warm place for about 1 hour, until doubled in bulk.

5. Punch down the dough and roll out to fit an oiled

Step 1 Scoop the flesh of the sun-dried tomatoes out of the peels, using a teaspoon.

Step 5 Roll the dough out to fit an oiled baking pan and press the dough out to fill the corners.

10 x 6-inch or 9-inch square baking pan. Press the dough out to fill the corners then cover and leave in a warm place for another 30 minutes, or until well risen.

6. Score the dough diagonally using a sharp knife. Brush the dough with the remaining olive oil and scatter the surface with coarse sea salt. Bake in a preheated 400°F oven for 30 minutes, until a pale golden brown, then cool on a wire rack.

Cook's Notes

Time
Preparation takes about 2½ hours, cooking takes 30 minutes.

Cook's Tip
While it is not essential to peel the sun-dried tomatoes the skin can be rather tough.

PUMPKIN AND CHEESE BREAD

This moist, savory bread is an ideal way of using up some of the flesh from your Halloween pumpkin.

MAKES 1 LARGE LOAF

1 ounce compressed yeast
1¼ cups lukewarm water
4 cups bread flour or all-purpose flour
3½ cups whole-wheat flour
1 tablespoon salt
1¼ cups pumpkin purée
¾ cup grated Cheddar cheese
½ cup pumpkinseeds
2 tablespoons olive oil

1. Crumble the yeast into ⅔ cup of the warm water and leave for 3-4 minutes, then stir well to completely dissolve the yeast.

2. Mix together the flours and salt in a large bowl and make a well in the center. Pour in the pumpkin purée.

Step 4 Knead the dough on a lightly floured surface.

Step 5 Work the cheese and most of the pumpkinseeds into the dough.

3. Add the yeast liquid to the bowl with as much of the remaining water as necessary to form a soft but manageable dough.

4. Knead the dough for about 10 minutes on a lightly floured surface until smooth and elastic. Return the dough to the bowl, cover and leave for about 45 minutes in a warm place, until doubled in bulk.

5. Punch the dough down and work in the cheese and most of the pumpkinseeds. Shape the dough into a large round and place it on a floured baking sheet. Cover and leave to rise for another 30-40 minutes.

6. Brush the loaf with the olive oil, then scatter the remaining pumpkinseeds over the bread, pressing them lightly into the surface. Bake in a preheated 425°F oven for 35 minutes, then cool on a wire rack.

Cook's Notes

Time
Preparation takes about 2 hours, cooking takes 35 minutes.

Variation
Add 2 tablespoons freshly chopped lovage with the cheese.

Preparation
If you don't want to use canned pumpkin purée, purée your own pumpkin or substitute your favorite winter squash.

ZUCCHINI BREAD

This attractively speckled loaf makes super double-decker sandwiches and can also be used for the base of open sandwiches. Make certain that all the moisture is extracted from the zucchinis, so that the dough does not become too moist and sticky.

MAKES 2 LOAVES

1 pound zucchinis, washed and trimmed
Fine sea salt
6 cups bread flour or all-purpose flour
1 teaspoon salt
1 ounce compressed yeast
1¼ cups lukewarm water
Beaten egg to glaze

1. Grate the zucchinis coarsely, either in a food processor or by hand grater. Squeeze out any excess liquid then layer the zucchinis in a colander with salt and leave to stand for at least 1 hour.

2. Rinse the zucchinis thoroughly under cold running water, squeeze them as dry as possible in your hands and add them to the flour in a large mixing bowl. Stir in the measured salt.

3. Crumble the yeast into the water and stir until dissolved, then pour the liquid into the flour and work to a soft but manageable dough.

4. Knead thoroughly on a lightly floured surface until smooth and elastic – as you work the dough the zucchinis may produce more water, so be prepared to add a little more flour during the kneading.

5. Place the dough in a clean bowl, cover and leave in a warm place for about 1 hour, until doubled in bulk.

6. Punch the dough down and knead lightly on a floured

Step 1 Layer the grated zucchinis in a colander with salt and leave for at least 1 hour.

Step 2 Rinse the zucchinis, squeeze them dry, then mix them into the flour.

surface. Divide the dough into two and shape the pieces to fit two oiled 8½ x 4½ x 2½-inch loaf pans. Cover and leave in a warm place for 30-45 minutes, until well risen.

7. Brush the breads with the beaten egg. Bake in a preheated 425°F oven for 30 minutes, until the loaves are golden brown and sound hollow when tapped underneath. Cool on a wire rack.

Cook's Notes

Time
Preparation takes 2½-2¾ hours, cooking takes 30 minutes.

Cook's Tip
To extract as much water as possible from the zucchinis, squeeze them between two plates or wrap in a cloth.

POPPY SEED AND ANCHOVY FOCACCIA

Focaccias are our favorite Italian breads to make – there are so many combinations of flavorings to use in the basic dough. In this recipe anchovies add a pronounced saltiness to the dough and the poppy seeds give an unusual crunchy texture.

MAKES 1 LOAF

1 ounce compressed yeast
1 cup lukewarm water
4 cups bread flour or all-purpose flour
1 teaspoon salt
⅓ cup poppy seeds
2 ounces canned anchovy fillets, chopped
¼ cup olive oil

To finish
3-4 canned anchovy fillets
¼ cup olive oil
Coarse sea salt

1. Crumble the yeast into the warm water and leave for 3-4 minutes, then stir to completely dissolve the yeast.

2. Mix the flour, salt, poppy seeds and anchovies and

Step 4 Roll out the dough to fit the baking pan.

Step 4 Make a dozen or so slits in the dough and fill each on with little slivers of anchovy.

oil in a bowl. Add the yeast liquid and mix to a dough.

3. Knead the dough well on a lightly floured surface until it is smooth and elastic. Return to the bowl, cover and leave in a warm place for 1½-2 hours, until the dough has doubled in bulk.

4. Lightly oil a shallow baking pan about 8 x 12 inches or 9 inches square. Punch the dough down and roll it out to fit the pan. To finish the bread, make a dozen or so slits in the dough and fill each one with little slivers of anchovy. Cover and leave in a warm place for about 30 minutes.

5. Brush the olive oil over the loaf and sprinkle it generously with coarse sea salt. Bake in a preheated 425°F oven for 25-30 minutes or until the loaf sounds hollow when tapped underneath. Cool on a wire rack.

Cook's Notes

Time
Preparation takes 2½-3 hours, cooking takes 25-30 minutes.

Cook's Tip
Turn the loaf over carefully when checking to see if it is cooked, so as not to break the garnish. It will brown more than regular focaccia because of the saltiness of the anchovies.

WALNUT BREAD

This is a light French-style bread. We often find walnut bread to be rather tasteless so this recipe contains honey and nutmeg to bring out the flavor of the nuts.

MAKES 1 LOAF

½ ounce compressed yeast
⅔ cup lukewarm water
1 cup walnut pieces
2 cups bread flour or all-purpose flour
1⅔ cup whole-wheat flour
1 teaspoon salt
⅔ cup milk
1 tablespoon clear honey
1 teaspoon grated nutmeg
2 tablespoons olive oil

1. Crumble the yeast into the warm water and leave for 3-4 minutes, then stir to completely dissolve the yeast. Finely chop the walnuts.

2. Mix together the flours, salt and walnuts in a large bowl. Heat the milk, honey and nutmeg together in a saucepan until just lukewarm.

3. Add the yeast and milk mixtures to the flour with the olive oil, mix well and bring together into a firm but manageable dough.

4. Turn out onto a lightly floured surface and knead until smooth and elastic. Put the dough in a bowl, cover and leave for about 1 hour in a warm place, until doubled in bulk.

5. Punch the dough down lightly then shape into a

Step 1 Finely chop the walnuts.

Step 2 Add the warm milk and yeast mixture to the flour and walnuts.

round loaf and place on a floured baking sheet. Leave to rise again for about 30 minutes.

6. Dust the loaf lightly with some whole-wheat flour then bake in a preheated 425°F oven for 30 minutes. Cool on a wire rack.

Cook's Notes

Time
Preparation takes about 2 hours, cooking takes 30 minutes.

Cook's Tip
For a dinner party, make 2 small loaves and cook them for about 20 minutes – small slices are much better than rolls for this bread.

Preparation
Use freshly grated nutmeg if possible.

CHEESY MALTED GRAIN ROLLS

Malted grain flour, a textured variation on whole-wheat flour,
produces a lovely nutty flavored bread.

MAKES 12 ROLLS

½ ounce compressed yeast
1¼ cups lukewarm milk
3 cups plus 1 tablespoon malted grain flour
2 cups bread flour or all-purpose flour
1 teaspoon salt
3 tablespoons olive oil
⅔ cup lukewarm water
1 cup grated Cheddar cheese

1. Crumble the yeast into the milk and leave for 3-4 minutes then stir to completely dissolve the yeast.

2. Mix the flours and salt together in a bowl and make a well in the center. Pour in the oil and yeast liquid and add as much of the warm water as required to mix to a soft, manageable dough.

3. Turn out onto a lightly floured surface and knead the dough thoroughly until smooth and elastic. Return it to the bowl, cover and leave for about 1 hour in a warm place, until doubled in bulk.

4. Punch the dough down, adding half the cheese, then divide into 12 pieces. Shape the dough pieces into rolls by rolling them under the palm of your hand in a circular motion, pressing down firmly. Continue rolling the dough, gradually raising your hand while curling in your fingers, until the rolls are smooth and round. Place the rolls on floured baking sheets. Cover and leave for another 30-40 minutes, until well risen.

5. Top the rolls with the remaining grated cheese then bake in a preheated 425°F oven for about 20 minutes. Transfer the rolls to a wire rack to cool.

Step 4 Divide the dough into 12 pieces then shape into rolls.

Step 5 Top the rolls with the remaining grated cheese.

Cook's Notes

🕐 **Time**
Preparation takes about 2 hours, cooking takes about 20 minutes.

❄ **Serving Idea**
Use these rolls for pack lunches and picnics.

PESTO STICK

Pesto, a sauce of basil, olive oil, pine nuts, garlic and Parmesan, is one of
our favorite seasonings. We use it in this recipe to make a colorful,
flavor-packed swirl in a stick-shaped loaf.

MAKES 1 LOAF

½ ounce compressed yeast
½ cup lukewarm water
2 cups bread flour or all-purpose flour
Large pinch of salt
3 tablespoons olive oil
2 tablespoons pesto sauce

1. Crumble the yeast into the warm water and leave for 3-4 minutes then stir well until completely dissolved.

2. Mix the flour and salt in a bowl, then add the yeast liquid with 2 tablespoons of the olive oil. Mix together then turn onto a floured surface and knead into a smooth pliable dough.

3. Return to a bowl, cover and leave for 1 hour in a warm place, until doubled in bulk.

4. Punch the dough down gently, then roll it out into an oblong about 7 x 10 inches. Spread with the pesto sauce, leaving a narrow margin all around the edge.

5. Roll the dough up like a jelly roll, starting from one of the long sides and place it on a floured baking tray, seam-side downwards. Cover and leave to rise for another 20 minutes.

Step 4 Spread the dough with the pesto sauce.

Step 5 Roll up the dough from one of the long sides.

6. Brush the remaining olive oil over the loaf, slash the surface with a sharp blade or a knife and bake in a preheated 400°F oven for 30 minutes until the loaf is golden brown. Cool on a wire rack.

Cook's Notes

Time
Preparation takes about 1¾-2 hours, cooking takes 30 minutes.

Variation
Use a sun-dried tomato or olive paste in place of the pesto.

Cook's Tip
This makes a delicious accompaniment to pasta and all Italian dishes.

BACON AND CHEESE BREAD

This savory loaf is an ideal bread for a Saturday lunch with a steaming bowl of soup.

MAKES 1 LARGE LOAF

¾ ounce compressed yeast
Scant 2 cups lukewarm water
2 cups bread flour or all-purpose flour
2 teaspoons salt
1 tablespoon olive oil
3½ cups whole-wheat flour
4 strips bacon
1 cup grated Cheddar cheese

1. Crumble the yeast into the warm water in a large mixing bowl and stir until dissolved. Add the bread flour or all-purpose flour and mix to a creamy consistency. Cover and leave in a warm place for 30 minutes until the mixture is bubbling and frothy.

2. Add the salt and the olive oil and work in the whole-wheat flour. Turn the dough out onto a lightly floured

Step 1 Leave the mixture in a warm place until bubbling and frothy.

Step 6 Press the remaining strip of bacon into the top of the dough.

surface and knead for about 10 minutes until it is smooth and pliable.

3. Return the dough to the bowl, cover and leave for 45 minutes-1 hour, until the dough has doubled in bulk.

4. Broil the bacon until cooked but not too crisp, then chop all but one strip into small pieces.

5. Punch down the dough and work in the chopped bacon with most of the cheese. Shape into a round, flat loaf and place on a floured baking sheet. Cover and leave to proof for about 30 minutes.

6. Scatter the loaf with the remaining cheese just before baking and press the remaining bacon onto the dough. Bake in a preheated 425°F oven for 45 minutes or until the bread sounds hollow when tapped underneath. Cool on a wire rack.

Cook's Notes

Time
Preparationtakes about 2½ hours, cooking takes 45 minutes.

Variation
Chop 6-8 halves of sun-dried tomatoes, and use in place of the chopped bacon.

SAUSAGE BRIOCHE

Hot dogs are not the only way of eating a sausage in bread, and this variation is infinitely preferable to our tastebuds! Use any long thin sausage of a diameter up to 2 inches. We like to use a strong French garlic sausage.

MAKES 1 LARGE LOAF

Half recipe of brioche dough (see page 140)
1 piece of cooked or smoked sausage, weighing about
   1 pound
1 egg, beaten with a pinch of salt

1. Make up the brioche dough as directed, leaving it overnight or for a minimum of 6 hours in the refrigerator for the second, cold rising.

2. Punch the dough down and roll it out until it is large enough to wrap around the sausage.

Step 3 Wrap the dough around the sausage to enclose it completely.

Step 4 Place the loaf on a floured baking sheet, sitting it on the join in the dough.

3. Remove any wrapping or skin from the sausage, place the meat on the dough and wrap the dough around it to enclose it completely, sealing the ends.

4. Place the loaf, join-side downwards, on a floured baking sheet. Cover and leave in a warm place for 45 minutes – this is the third rising.

5. Brush the dough with the egg glaze and bake in a preheated 350°F oven for 30-35 minutes, until dark golden brown. Cool on a wire rack before eating warm.

Cook's Notes

Time
Preparation of the dough takes 2-2½ hours plus overnight rising, then another 1 hour the next day. Cooking takes 30-35 minutes.

Cook's Tip
Lift the loaf carefully to prevent the sausage from falling through the bottom of the bread.

Serving Idea
This makes ideal picnic food.

ROMAN FOCACCIA

This is a classic Italian bread, topped with thinly sliced raw onion
which bakes to a golden brown in the oven.

MAKES 1 LOAF

1 ounce compressed yeast
1 cup lukewarm water
4 cups bread flour or all-purpose flour
1 teaspoon salt
⅓ cup fruity olive oil
2 large onions
1 large sprig fresh rosemary
Coarse salt

1. Crumble the yeast into the warm water and leave for 3-4 minutes, then stir to completely dissolve the yeast.

2. Mix the flour and salt together and make a well in the center. Add ¼ cup of the olive oil and the yeast liquid and mix together into a manageable dough.

3. Turn out onto a lightly floured surface and knead until smooth and elastic. Return the dough to the bowl, cover and leave in a warm place for about 1 hour, until doubled in bulk.

4. Slice the onions very thinly and place in cold water. Leave to soak for at least 30 minutes.

Step 4 Place the sliced onions in cold water to soak for at least 30 minutes.

5. Punch the dough down and roll it out to fit an oiled baking pan about 16 x 10 inches. Lift the dough into the pan, pressing it well into the corners. Cover and leave in a warm place to rise for 20-30 minutes. Drain the onion slices and dry thoroughly.

6. Brush the dough with the remaining oil then top with the onion slices. Strip the rosemary leaves from the stalk and chop finely. Scatter them over the onions with some coarse sea salt.

7. Bake in a preheated 425°F oven for 20-30 minutes, until the onions are soft and the bread is a pale golden brown. Cool on a wire rack before eating warm.

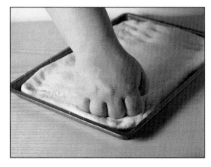

Step 5 Roll out the dough to fit the baking pan and press it into the corners.

Step 6 Scatter the chopped rosemary over the onion topping.

Cook's Notes

Time
Preparation takes about 2¼ hours, cooking takes 20-30 minutes.

Variation
Sprinkle ¼ cup freshly grated Parmesan over the onion topping before baking.

SPINACH AND OLIVE OIL BREAD

This is a wonderful loaf to take on picnics as it is almost a meal in itself!

MAKES 1 LARGE LOAF

Bread
1 ounce compressed yeast
1 cup lukewarm water
4 cups bread flour or all-purpose flour
2 teaspoons salt
6 tablespoons olive oil

Filling
8 ounces spinach
¼ cup butter
1 small onion, finely chopped
1 clove garlic, minced
3 tablespoons sesame seeds
Salt and freshly ground black pepper
1 cup finely diced feta cheese
1 tablespoon freshly chopped parsley

Topping
2 tablespoons olive oil
Coarse sea salt

Step 4 Finely chop the spinach for the filling.

Step 4 Add the cheese to the cooked spinach when it has cooled.

1. Crumble the yeast into the warm water, leave for 3-4 minutes then stir until completely dissolved.

2. Mix the flour and salt in a bowl, add the yeast with the oil and mix to a soft, manageable dough. Turn onto a floured surface and knead until smooth and elastic.

3. Place the dough in a bowl, cover and leave in a warm place for about 1 hour, until doubled in bulk.

4. Prepare the filling while the dough is rising. Wash and finely chop the spinach. Melt the butter in a saucepan and cook the onion and garlic until soft. Add the spinach and cook briefly until it wilts, then stir in the sesame seeds and season well. Leave to cool then add the feta cheese and chopped parsley.

5. Punch the dough down and divide it into two equal pieces. Roll each one out into an oval shape about 7 x 10 inches. Place one piece of dough on a floured baking sheet and pile the filling into the center. Cover with the remaining dough and seal the edges together. Cover and leave to rise for 20-30 minutes.

6. To finish the loaf, drizzle the olive oil over the top – it may run off creating an attractive pattern. Sprinkle with some coarse salt and bake for 30 minutes, until golden brown. Carefully transfer to a wire rack to cool.

Cook's Notes

Time
Preparation takes about 1¾-2 hours, cooking takes 30 minutes.

Variation
Add chopped toasted hazelnuts and blue cheese to the filling in place of the sesame seeds and feta.

Cook's Tip
Take care when handling the bread fresh from the oven, the filling is quite heavy so support the bottom of the loaf.

OLIVE BREAD

This is a very rich dough, made with almost equal quantities of olive oil and water. Because of the weight of the oil we use 1 ounce of compressed yeast for this loaf, despite the fact that it is made with just 4 cups of flour.

MAKES 1 LOAF

1 ounce compressed yeast
1 cup lukewarm water
4 cups bread flour or all-purpose flour
1 teaspoon salt
⅔ cup good fruity olive oil
1 cup stuffed green olives, drained

1. Crumble the yeast into half the warm water and leave for 3-4 minutes, then stir to completely dissolve the yeast.

2. Mix together the flour and salt in a bowl and make a well in the center.

3. Add ½ cup of the olive oil and the yeast liquid, then mix to a manageable dough. Add the rest of the water as necessary.

4. Knead the dough thoroughly on a floured surface until smooth and elastic, then return the dough to the bowl. Cover and leave in a warm place for 1-1½ hours, until doubled in bulk.

5. Reserve two whole olives. Finely chop the majority of the remaining olives and coarsely chop the rest – this will give a variety of pieces in the finished bread.

6. Punch the dough down lightly, then work in the chopped olives. Shape the dough into a round loaf and place it on a floured baking sheet or in a round cake

Step 5 Finely chop the majority of the olives.

pan. Press the whole olives into the top of the bread. Cover with a damp cloth and leave to proof for about 30 minutes, until doubled in bulk.

7. Brush the loaf with the remaining oil then bake in a preheated 425°F oven for 30-35 minutes until the base sounds hollow when tapped and the loaf is a pale golden color. Cool on a wire rack.

Step 6 Press the reserved whole olives into the top of the bread.

Cook's Notes

Time
Preparation takes 2¼-2¾ hours, cooking takes 30-35 minutes.

Cook's Tip
The dough may become sticky while the olives are being worked in, so have a little extra flour to hand.

Preparation
Use pimiento or almond stuffed olives.

MUSHROOM BRIOCHE

Filled brioche are a heavenly indulgence! Although the dough is quite sweet it combines perfectly with this mushroom filling to make a delightful lunch or picnic bread.

MAKES 1 LARGE LOAF

Half recipe of brioche dough (see page 140)

Filling
½ ounce butter
¼ cup flour
⅔ cup milk
Salt and freshly ground black pepper
Freshly grated nutmeg to taste
6 ounces mushrooms, finely chopped
½ cup finely grated Cheddar cheese

1 egg, beaten with a pinch of salt, for glazing

1. Make up the brioche dough as directed, leaving it overnight or for at least 6 hours, in the refrigerator for the second, cold rising.

2. Prepare the mushroom filling. Melt the butter, stir in the flour and cook for 1 minute, then gradually add the milk. Bring the sauce to a boil, stirring all the time – it will become very thick.

3. Season the sauce with salt, pepper and nutmeg. Stir in the mushrooms and cheese and leave to cool.

Step 2 Gradually add the milk to the sauce for the filling.

4. Punch the dough down and divide it into two. Roll out half the dough and use it to line the bottom of a deep 10-inch round cake pan. Cover the dough with the mushroom mixture, leaving a narrow band free of the filling all the way around the edge. Roll out the rest of the dough and use to cover the filling.

5. Press the edges of the dough circles together to seal them. Cover and proof in a warm place for 45 minutes – this is the third rising.

6. Brush the dough with the egg glaze and bake in a preheated 350°F oven for 30-35 minutes, until dark golden brown. Cool briefly on a wire rack before cutting into wedges and eating warm.

Step 4 Cover the dough with the mushroom mixture, leaving a gap all the way around the edge.

Step 5 Press the edges of the dough together to seal them.

Cook's Notes

Time
Preparation takes 2-2½ hours plus overnight rising, then another 1½ hours the next day. Cooking takes 30-35 minutes.

Variation
Use a selection of mushrooms for the filling and omit the cheese to let the mushroom flavor dominate.

BASIL AND GOAT'S CHEESE FOCACCIA

These are wonderful breads to serve with an appetizer at a dinner party. They will puff up slightly around the cheese filling, which is absolutely delicious.

MAKES 8 INDIVIDUAL LOAVES

¾ ounce compressed yeast
1½ cups lukewarm water
6 cups bread flour or all-purpose flour
1½ teaspoons salt
6 tablespoons olive oil
16-20 fresh basil leaves
7 ounces goat's cheese (plain or with garlic and herbs)
Coarse sea salt

1. Crumble the yeast into the water, leave for 3-4 minutes then stir until the yeast is completely dissolved.

2. Mix the flour and salt in a bowl, then add 5 tablespoons of the olive oil and the yeast liquid and mix well.

3. Turn onto a lightly floured surface and knead until the dough is smooth and elastic. Cover and leave to rise in a warm place for about 1½ hours, until doubled in bulk.

4. Finely chop the basil leaves and mix with the goat's cheese, crumbling them together coarsely with a fork. Punch down the dough and divide it into eight equal pieces.

Step 4 Mix the chopped basil and goat's cheese, crumbling them together with a fork.

Step 5 Enclose a little of the filling in each circle of dough.

Step 7 Brush the focaccias with the remaining oil and sprinkle them with coarse sea salt.

5. Flatten each piece of dough into a circle, place some of the cheese and basil mixture on each one and enclose the filling in the dough.

6. Roll out each focaccia into a circle about 3-4 inches across, taking care not to let the cheese break through the surface.

7. Place the focaccias on floured baking sheets, brush with the remaining olive oil and sprinkle with coarse sea salt. Cover and leave for 1 hour.

8. Bake the focaccias in a preheated 350°F oven for 30 minutes, then cool slightly before serving warm.

Cook's Notes

Time
Preparation takes about 3½ hours, cooking takes 30 minutes.

Variation
Add finely shredded sun-dried tomatoes to the cheese filling.

Cook's Tip
Use a fresh, soft goat's cheese for this recipe.

SAGE AND ORANGE BREAD

These breads are shaped like the traditional fougasses of Provençe –
they are flat and slit in a herringbone pattern.

MAKES 8 SMALL BREADS

½ ounce compressed yeast
½ cup warm water
6 cups all-purpose flour
1 teaspoon salt
Grated rind and juice of 1 orange
12 fresh sage leaves, finely chopped
¼ cup Spanish olive oil
2 large eggs, beaten

1. Crumble the yeast into the warm water and leave for 3-4 minutes, then stir to completely dissolve the yeast.

2. Mix the flour, salt, orange rind and sage together in a large bowl and make a well in the center. Add the yeast liquid with 3 tablespoons of the olive oil, the eggs, orange juice and sufficient extra water to form a soft but manageable dough.

3. Turn the dough out onto a floured surface and knead until smooth and elastic. Place in a bowl, cover and leave in a warm place for 1 hour, until doubled in bulk.

4. Punch the dough down then divide it into 8. Roll out each piece into an oval about ½-inch thick. Place the breads on floured baking sheets, cover and leave for another 45 minutes, until well risen and puffy.

Step 4 Place the oval breads on floured baking sheets.

5. Brush the breads with the remaining olive oil then cut 8 or 9 slits in each, in a herringbone design. Do not cut through the edges of the bread.

6. Bake in a preheated 400°F oven for 20 minutes until golden brown, then transfer to a wire rack to cool.

Step 5 Make 8 or 9 slits in each bread in a herringbone pattern. Do not cut through the edges of the bread.

Cook's Notes

Time
Preparation takes about 2-2¼ hours, cooking takes 20 minutes.

Variation
To make a sweet version, omit the sage and add ½ cup chopped candied peels to the dough.

Cook's Tip
Spanish olive oil combines particularly well with oranges.

PIZZA DOUGH

You either like thin, crusty pizzas or the deep-pan variety. We prefer the former and make two bases from this amount of dough. A good pizza dough is made with good olive oil.

MAKES 2 LARGE THIN PIZZA BASES

½ ounce compressed yeast
¼ cup warm water
2 cups all-purpose flour
½ teaspoon salt
3 tablespoons fruity olive oil

1. Crumble the yeast into the warm water and leave for 3-4 minutes, then stir to completely dissolve the yeast.

2. Mix the flour and salt together and make a well in the center. Add 2 tablespoons of the oil and all the yeast liquid and mix to a soft but manageable dough, adding extra water as necessary.

3. Turn the dough out and knead it thoroughly until smooth and elastic. Divide the dough into two and roll out or shape by mid-air folds (see introduction) into two rounds of about 10 inches. Place on floured baking sheets or in pizza pans, cover and leave in a warm place for 15-20 minutes.

4. Brush the dough with the remaining olive oil then add the toppings of your choice.

5. Bake the pizzas in a preheated 425°F oven for 15

Step 2 Add 2 tbsps of the oil and the yeast liquid.

Step 3 Roll the dough out or shape by mid-air folds into rounds.

minutes, until the topping is heated through and the base is cooked.

Cook's Notes

Time
Preparation takes about ¾-1 hour, cooking takes 15 minutes.

Variation
One deep-pan pizza can be made from the same quantity of dough and will require 25-30 minutes cooking time.

Chapter 3
Quick Breads

IRISH SODA BREAD

Traditionally the Irish are daily bakers and this is their everyday bread.
It is quick to mix and bake and requires no kneading. We always make a small loaf
of this bread to eat it all fresh. Double the quantities if you wish, and increase
the cooking times accordingly.

MAKES 1 SMALL LOAF

2 cups all-purpose flour
½ teaspoon salt
1 teaspoon bicarbonate of soda (baking soda)
½ teaspoon cream of tartar
1 tablespoon butter
¾ cup buttermilk

Step 2 Add the buttermilk and mix to a soft dough with a metal spatula.

Step 1 Cut the butter into the dry ingredients.

1. Mix the flour, salt, bicarbonate of soda and cream of tartar together in a bowl, then cut in the butter.

2. Pour in the buttermilk and mix to a soft dough with a metal spatula. Turn out onto a floured surface, and shape into a round – do not knead the dough.

3. Place on a floured baking sheet and score a cross in the top of the loaf using a sharp knife. Sprinkle lightly with flour.

4. Bake in a preheated 425°F oven for 10 minutes, then reduce the temperature to 400°F and bake for another 10 minutes. Allow to cool on a wire rack.

Cook's Notes

Time
Preparation takes 10-15 minutes, cooking takes about 20 minutes.

Cook's Tip
To make a light soda bread it is important to mix it as quickly and lightly as possible.

Serving Idea
Break the bread into four sections, split in half and spread with butter.

IRISH SODA FARLS

Traditional Irish cooked breakfasts take some beating: sausages, bacon, eggs and, the sublime final touch, freshly cooked soda farls. These are triangular soda breads cooked on a griddle, or in a heavy-based skillet.

MAKES 4-6

2 cups all-purpose flour
1 teaspoon salt
1 teaspoon bicarbonate of soda (baking soda)
⅔ cup buttermilk

1. Preheat a griddle or a heavy-based skillet.

2. Sift the flour, salt and bicarbonate of soda into a

Step 3 Roll out the dough on a lightly floured surface.

Step 3 Cut into 4-6 segments.

mixing bowl, then add the buttermilk and mix with a metal spatula to form a soft but workable dough. Do not overwork the mixture.

3. Turn out onto a lightly floured surface and roll out into a circle about ½-inch thick. Cut the dough into four or six segments.

4. Cook on the griddle for 5-6 minutes on each side, then serve with a traditional cooked breakfast.

Cook's Notes

🕐 **Time**
Preparation takes about 10 minutes, cooking takes 10-12 minutes.

🎩 **Cook's Tip**
Do not overheat the griddle or the farls will burn on the outside before they are cooked through in the center.

WHEATEN IRISH SODA BREAD

Traditional soda breads have a glorious yellow color and a very biscuit-like texture.
This wheaten loaf is more like a traditional bread, and is our favorite soda bread.

MAKES 1 LOAF

2 cups all-purpose flour
Scant 1 cup whole-wheat flour
1½ teaspoons bicarbonate of soda (baking soda)
1⅓ cups bran
2 teaspoons superfine sugar
Pinch of salt
Scant 2 cups buttermilk

1. Lightly grease a deep 7-inch round cake pan.

2. Mix the flours, bicarbonate of soda, bran, sugar and salt together in a large mixing bowl. Make a well in the center and pour in the buttermilk.

3. Mix the ingredients together well using a metal spatula. No kneading is necessary with this type of dough. Spoon the dough into the prepared cake pan and smooth the top.

4. Bake the soda bread in a preheated 400°F oven for 40-45 minutes, then turn out and cool on a wire rack.

Step 2 Pour the buttermilk into the dry ingredients.

Step 3 Spoon the dough into the prepared cake pan and smooth the top.

Cook's Notes

Time
Preparation takes about 15 minutes, cooking takes 40-45 minutes.

Cook's Tip
Do not overmix the bread or it will become heavy.

Variation
Add some golden raisins to the dry ingredients before mixing.

CREAMY CORN BREAD

This is a delicious savory loaf – the addition of dried bell pepper flakes really lifts the flavor of what might otherwise be a rather bland mixture.

MAKES 1 LOAF

1 cup fine yellow cornmeal
1 cup all-purpose flour
¼ cup superfine sugar
2½ teaspoons baking powder (bread soda)
2 tablespoons dried bell pepper flakes
Large pinch of salt
2 large eggs
1½ cups creamed corn
⅔ cup milk
⅔ cup heavy cream
½ cup butter, melted

1. Lightly oil an 8 or 9-inch round cake pan.

Step 2 Mix all the dry ingredients together in a large bowl.

Step 4 Whip the egg whites until stiff then fold them into the mixture.

2. Mix all the dry ingredients together in a large bowl.

3. Separate the eggs and combine the yolks with the corn, milk, cream and melted butter. Pour the liquid into the cornmeal mixture and stir thoroughly but not too vigorously, to retain the texture of the corn.

4. Whip the egg whites until stiff, then fold them into the mixture. Pour into the oiled cake pan and smooth the top over.

5. Bake in a preheated 375°F oven for 45-50 minutes, until lightly browned and set. Test the corn bread by inserting a wooden toothpick into the center – if it comes out clean, the bread is cooked.

6. Allow to cool slightly before removing the loaf from the pan to a wire rack. Serve sliced, warm or cold.

Cook's Notes

Time
Preparation takes about 15 minutes, cooking takes 45-50 minutes.

Serving Idea
Serve with a selection of cheeses for an informal weekend lunch or as an alternative to potatoes.

BOSTON BROWN BREAD

These traditional East Coast breads are steamed in cans to make individual loaves.

MAKES 6 SMALL LOAVES

2 cups fine cornmeal
1¾ cups whole-wheat flour
1 cup bread flour or all-purpose flour
Pinch of salt
6 tablespoons molasses
1 teaspoon bicarbonate of soda (baking soda)
Scant 2 cups cold water

1. Rinse out six 14-ounce food cans, dry them thoroughly and oil generously.

2. Mix the dry ingredients together in a large bowl.

3. Mix the molasses, bicarbonate of soda and water together then pour the mixture into the flour. Mix just until well blended.

4. Spoon the bread mixture into the prepared cans, filling them about half full.

5. Cover the tops of the cans tightly with buttered or oiled foil, tying it on securely. Place the cans on a rack in a deep saucepan. Pour enough boiling water around the cans to come about halfway up their sides.

6. Cover the pan and simmer the bread for 3-4 hours. Check the level of the water from time to time and add

Step 1 Generously oil the cans.

more boiling water as necessary during cooking.

7. The bread is ready when a wooden toothpick inserted into the center comes out clean. Turn out of the cans onto a wire rack to cool.

Step 5 Tie the foil tightly and securely over the cans.

Cook's Notes

Time
Preparation takes 15 minutes, cooking takes 3-4 hours.

Variation
Use rye flour in place of the cornmeal and steam as one large loaf, in a bombe mold, for about 6 hours.

Serving Idea
Serve with Boston baked beans, as the traditional accompaniment, or serve spread with butter or cream cheese.

ONION AND TOMATO QUICK BREAD

This quick bread is ideal to serve with soup or winter salads.

MAKES 1 LOAF

1 medium onion
3 tomatoes
2 cups self-rising whole-wheat flour
½ teaspoon salt
1 teaspoon dry mustard
½ teaspoon paprika
2 tablespoons freshly chopped parsley
2 tablespoons butter
1 large egg, beaten
½ cup milk

Step 2 Coarsely grate the onion.

1. Lightly oil an 8½ x 4½ x 2½-inch bread pan.

2. Coarsely grate the onion by hand or in a food processor. Peel the tomatoes by covering with boiling water for 30 seconds. Drain, rinse in cold water and pull off the peel. Cut the tomatoes in half, scoop out the seeds and chop the flesh.

3. Mix all the dry ingredients and the parsley together in a bowl and cut in the butter. Stir in the grated onion and the chopped tomatoes then make a well in the center. Add the egg and milk and mix to form a soft biscuit consistency.

4. Spoon the mixture into the oiled pan then bake in a preheated 375°F oven for 40 minutes, until golden brown.

5. Cool the loaf for a few minutes in the pan, then turn out onto a wire rack to cool.

Cook's Notes

Time
Preparation takes about 10 minutes, cooking takes about 40 minutes.

Variation
Add finely diced green bell pepper to the loaf instead of the tomato.

BEER AND FRUIT BRAN BREAD

This high-fiber tea bread is made in an instant – most quick breads have a smooth crumb but this one is full of texture and flavor.

MAKES 1 LOAF

1 cup bran
1 cup (lightly packed) brown sugar
⅓ cup each currants, raisins and golden raisins
1 cup dark beer
¼ cup butter, melted
1½ cups self-rising flour
1 teaspoon baking powder (bread soda)
½ cup walnut pieces

1. Lightly oil an 8½ x 4½ x 2½-inch bread pan.

2. Mix the bran, sugar and mixed dried fruits together in a bowl, add the beer and leave to stand for 10 minutes, so that the beer is absorbed.

3. Stir the melted butter into the soaked fruit, then add all the remaining ingredients and stir well. Turn into the prepared pan and smooth the top.

4. Bake in a preheated 350°F oven for about 1 hour, until a wooden toothpick inserted into the center of the loaf comes out clean.

Step 2 Mix the bran, sugar and dried fruits together in a bowl. Add the beer and leave to stand for 10 minutes.

5. Cool the loaf for a few minutes in the pan, then turn out onto a wire rack and leave until cold.

Step 3 Add the flour, baking powder and walnut pieces to the soaked fruit.

Cook's Notes

Time
Preparation takes 20-30 minutes, cooking takes about 1 hour.

Cook's Tip
Make sure you allow the fruit to soak up the beer or the final texture of the loaf will be soggy.

Serving Idea
Serve sliced and buttered or spread with cream cheese.

BANANA BREAD

This is an excellent way of using up over-ripe bananas.
MAKES 1 LARGE LOAF

½ cup unsalted butter
½ cup superfine sugar
1 large egg, beaten
1 teaspoon vanilla extract
2 cups all-purpose flour
1 tablespoon baking powder (bread soda)
½ teaspoon salt
Half a freshly grated nutmeg
1 pound (3-4 medium) ripe bananas
½ cup pecans, chopped
⅓ cup raisins

1. Lightly oil an 8½ x 4½ x 2½-inch bread pan.

2. Cream the butter and sugar together in a large bowl, then gradually beat in the egg and the vanilla extract.

3. Mix the flour, baking powder, salt and the nutmeg together in a bowl. Peel and mash the bananas.

4. Fold the flour and mashed bananas alternately into the creamed mixture, then add the chopped pecans and raisins.

5. Spoon the mixture into the prepared pan, and gently smooth the top.

6. Bake in a preheated 350°F oven for 1 hour, or until a wooden toothpick inserted into the center of the loaf comes out clean. Allow to cool slightly in the pan, then turn out onto a wire rack to cool completely.

Step 4 Fold the mashed bananas into the mixture.

Step 4 Add the chopped pecans, then the raisins.

Cook's Notes

🕐 **Time**
Prepration takes about 25 minutes, cooking takes about 1 hour.

🔪 **Variation**
Add the grated rind of a lemon in place of the nutmeg, and add 1 tablespoon lemon juice in place of the vanilla extract.

APRICOT BRAN BREAD

Bran is a very popular ingredient in quick breads, giving an unusual rough texture to the loaves. The apricots add only a little extra sweetness. For best results make these breads a day before they are required.

MAKES 2 LOAVES

2¼ cups whole-wheat flour
1¾ cups bran
¼ cup (firmly packed) brown sugar
1½ teaspoons bicarbonate of soda (baking soda)
½ teaspoon baking powder (bread soda)
½ teaspoon salt
¾ cup dried apricots, chopped
1¾ cups buttermilk
1 large egg, beaten
⅓ cup molasses

1. Lightly oil two 8½ x 4½ x 2½-inch bread pans.

Step 3 Whisk together the buttermilk, egg and molasses.

Step 3 Stir the mixture briefly until just mixed.

2. Mix together all the dry ingredients, including the apricots, in a large bowl.

3. Whisk together the buttermilk, egg and molasses then pour the mixture into the bowl. Stir briefly until just mixed, then spoon into the prepared pans and smooth the tops of the loaves.

4. Bake in a preheated 350°F oven for 1 hour, until a wooden toothpick inserted into the center of each loaf comes away clean. Cool for 10-15 minutes in the pans before turning out onto a wire rack to cool.

5. Cover the loaves with foil or plastic wrap and leave overnight before cutting.

Cook's Notes

⏱ Time
Preparation takes about 15 minutes, cooking takes about 1 hour.

❗ Watchpoint
Do not overmix the bread.

👨‍🍳 Cook's Tip
Leaving the loaves overnight before cutting them allows the flavor to develop.

BUCKWHEAT AND PRUNE LOAF

Buckwheat flour is very fine-grained and we use it mostly for pasta. However, it is a gluten-free flour and therefore suitable for making bread for those following a gluten-free diet. I like to add some prunes to the mixture for a bit of texture.

MAKES 1 SMALL LOAF

3 cups buckwheat flour
1 teaspoon salt
½ teaspoon baking powder (bread soda)
1½ teaspoons bicarbonate of soda (baking soda)
½ cup (lightly packed) brown sugar
1 cup pitted prunes, finely chopped
1¼ cups buttermilk

1. Lightly oil a 7-inch round cake pan.

2. Mix the flour, salt, baking powder, bicarbonate of soda and sugar together in a bowl. Stir in the finely chopped prunes.

3. Add the buttermilk and mix to a stiff dough using a metal spatula. Do not overmix.

4. Turn the mixture into the prepared pan and smooth the top over.

5. Bake in a preheated 350°F oven for 50-60 minutes. Cool briefly in the pan then turn onto a wire rack to cool completely.

Step 2 Stir in the chopped pitted prunes.

Step 3 Add the buttermilk and mix to a stiff dough using a metal spatula.

Cook's Notes

Time
Preparation takes about 10 minutes, cooking takes 50-60 minutes.

Variation
Add raisins or a mixture of raisins and chopped candied peels, instead of prunes.

Chapter 4
Enriched & Sweet Breads

CHALLAH

This is a traditional Jewish braided bread, baked for important festivals
throughout the year.

MAKES 2 LOAVES

¾ ounce compressed yeast
2 cups warm water
8 cups all-purpose flour
1 teaspoon salt
2 large eggs
2 tablespoons oil
¼ cup poppy seeds or sesame seeds

1. Crumble the yeast into ⅔ cup of the warm water. Leave for 3-4 minutes, then stir until completely dissolved. Cover and leave in a warm place until starting to froth, about 20 minutes.

2. Place the flour and salt in a bowl, make a well in the center and break one of the eggs into it. Add the yeast mixture with the oil and gradually stir the flour into the liquid. Gradually add enough of the remaining warm water to make a stiff dough.

Step 4 Braid three strips together to make each loaf.

Step 4 Tuck the ends neatly under the loaf.

3. Turn the dough out onto a lightly floured surface and knead until smooth and elastic. Place the dough in a clean bowl, cover and leave in a warm place for about 1½ hours, until doubled in bulk.

4. Punch the dough down and divide into 6 balls. Roll the balls between your hands into long strips of equal length about 1-inch wide. Braid 3 strips together for each loaf and place the loaves on floured baking sheets. Tuck the ends neatly underneath the loaves. Cover and leave in a warm place for about 45 minutes, until well risen.

5. Brush the loaves with the remaining beaten egg mixed with 2 tablespoons water and sprinkle with the seeds. Bake the loaves in a preheated 450°F oven for 15 minutes, then reduce the heat to 375°F and bake for another 40 minutes, or until golden brown. Cool on wire racks.

Cook's Notes

Time
Preparation takes 3-3½ hours, cooking takes 55 minutes.

Cook's Tip
Braiding takes some practice to get even – start the braiding very close to the top of the dough, so that it is tight and even along the whole of the length of the loaf. Sometimes it is easier to cross the dough strips over just a few times.

Variation
Add a pinch of powdered saffron to the water in step 2.

CARAWAY AND FENNEL SEED BREAD

This recipe is based on the Scandinavian favorite *Limpa* and is flavored with caraway and fennel seeds. The grated orange rind gives it a wonderful fragrance. This is a good breakfast bread.

MAKES 1 LOAF

1¼ cups water
1 teaspoon caraway seeds
1 tablespoon fennel seeds
¼ cup (firmly packed) brown sugar
Grated rind of 1 orange
½ ounce compressed yeast
3 cups bread flour or all-purpose flour
1 tablespoon olive oil
2 cups rye flour
1 teaspoon salt

1. Heat the water, caraway and fennel seeds, sugar and orange rind together until the sugar has dissolved and the mixture is just lukewarm. Crumble the yeast into the liquid off the heat and stir until dissolved.

2. Add the mixture to the bread flour or all-purpose flour with the olive oil and stir well. Cover and leave in a warm place for 30 minutes, until bubbling.

3. Stir the rye flour and salt into the ferment, then turn out onto a work surface and knead thoroughly, adding a little extra white flour if necessary to make a soft but manageable dough.

4. Place in a clean bowl, cover and leave in a warm place for about 1 hour, or until doubled in bulk.

5. Punch the dough down and knead lightly, then shape and place in an oiled 8½ x 4½ x 2½-inch bread pan. Cover and leave to proof again for 45 minutes, or until the dough has risen to the top of the pan.

6. Bake the bread in a preheated 425°F oven for 45 minutes. Allow to cool on a wire rack.

Step 1 Crumble the yeast into the liquid off the heat.

Step 3 Stir the rye flour and salt into the ferment.

Cook's Notes

Time
Preparation takes about 2¾ hours, cooking takes 45 minutes.

Variation
Ensure that you do not overheat the sugar and seed mixture – it is very easy to kill the yeast if the mixture is too hot.

MALT BREAD

Malt bread has always been a great teatime favorite. Commercial loaves are often very heavy and sticky but our loaf is much lighter, while keeping the lovely traditional malty flavor.

MAKES 1 LARGE LOAF

1 ounce compressed yeast
⅔ cup lukewarm water
4 cups all-purpose flour
1 teaspoon salt
⅔ cup mixed raisins and golden raisins
¼ cup malt extract
1 tablespoon molasses
2 tablespoons butter

Glaze
1 tablespoon superfine sugar
1 tablespoon water

1. Crumble the yeast into the warm water and leave for 3-4 minutes, then stir to completely dissolve the yeast.

2. Mix the flour, salt and dried fruits together in a bowl.

3. Warm the malt extract, molasses and butter gently in a saucepan until the butter is just melted – the mixture should be no more than lukewarm.

4. Mix the yeast liquid and malt mixture into the dry ingredients and work into a dough.

5. Knead thoroughly on a lightly floured surface and add a little more water if necessary to give a firm but sticky dough.

6. Place the dough in an oiled 8½ x 4½ x 2½-inch bread pan, cover and leave to rise until doubled in bulk, about 1½ hours.

Step 4 Mix the yeast liquid and malt mixture into the dry ingredients and work into a dough.

Step 5 Knead the firm but sticky dough thoroughly on a lightly floured surface.

7. Bake the loaf in a preheated 400°F oven for 30-40 minutes.

8. Make the glaze by boiling the sugar with the water to give a thick syrup. Brush the loaf with the glaze as soon as it comes out of the oven. Cool on a wire rack, then serve sliced and buttered.

Cook's Notes

Time
Preparation takes about 2 hours, cooking takes 30-40 minutes.

Variation
Add a little grated lemon or orange rind during mixing.

WHOLE-WHEAT AND HONEY LOAF

A country-style tea bread to serve with or without butter.
The pine nuts add a delicate sweetness to the loaf.

MAKES 1 LARGE LOAF

¾ ounce compressed yeast
1¾ cups warm water
3⅔ cups whole-wheat flour
¼ cup wheat germ
1 teaspoon salt
½ cup seedless raisins
½ cup pine nuts
3 tablespoons honey
1 tablespoon olive oil

1. Crumble the yeast into 1 cup of the warm water and leave for 3-4 minutes, then stir to completely dissolve the yeast.

2. Mix together the flour, wheat germ, salt, raisins and pine nuts then add the yeast liquid, honey, oil and the remaining water, mixing until the dough resembles a thick, dry fruit cake consistency.

3. Spoon the mixture into an oiled 8½ x 4½ x 2½-inch bread pan, cover and leave to rise in a warm place for about 30 minutes, until it has risen to the top of the pan.

4. Bake the loaf in a preheated 400°F oven for 30 minutes, then reduce the heat to 350°F, and continue

Step 2 Add the oil to the flour and wheat germ.

cooking for another 20 minutes. Turn out onto a wire rack to cool.

Step 3 Spoon the mixture into an oiled bread pan.

Cook's Notes

🕐 **Time**
Preparation takes 40-45 minutes, cooking takes 50 minutes.

◣ **Variation**
Use dates and walnuts in place of the raisins and pine nuts.

BRIOCHE

This is a very rich French bread dough, containing lots of butter and eggs. It is one dough that is much better mixed by machine than by hand.

MAKES 2 LOAVES

4½ cups bread flour or all-purpose flour
1 teaspoon salt
¼ cup superfine sugar
6 tablespoons lukewarm milk
1 ounce compressed yeast
5 large eggs, beaten
1 cup plus 2 tablespoons butter, softened
1 egg, beaten with a pinch of salt

1. Mix together the flour, salt and sugar. Pour the milk into the bowl of an electric mixer.

2. Crumble the yeast into the warm milk and add the beaten eggs and flour. Mix slowly until combined, using a general purpose beater. Add a spoonful more flour if necessary, then mix on a slightly higher speed for 10 minutes, or until the dough forms a ball around the beater and leaves the sides of the bowl.

3. Add the softened butter in small pieces, beating all the time, until the dough again leaves the sides of the

Step 2 Add the beaten eggs and flour to the yeast liquid.

Step 3 After adding the butter the dough will be sticky but firm, rather like chewing gum. This mixing is best done in a mixer.

bowl. It will be sticky yet firm, rather like chewing gum.

4. Shape the dough into a neat round on a floured surface, then return it to the bowl. Cover and leave in a warm place for about 1½-2 hours, until the dough has doubled in bulk.

5. Punch the dough down gently – this may be done in the mixer or on a lightly floured work surface. Return it to the bowl, cover tightly with plastic wrap and refrigerate overnight. This slow, cold rising makes the dough much easier to handle.

6. In the morning, punch the dough down again and divide it into two. Butter two brioche molds, bread pans or baking sheets and shape the dough as required. Cover and proof in a warm place for 45 minutes – this is the third rising.

7. Brush the dough carefully with the beaten egg and bake in a preheated 350°F oven for 30-35 minutes, until dark golden brown. The bases of the brioche should sound hollow when tapped. Cool on wire racks before serving warm.

Cook's Notes

Time
Preparation takes 2-2½ hours plus overnight rising, then another 1 hour the next morning. Cooking takes 30-35 minutes.

Cook's Tip
Brioche are traditionally cooked in fluted pans and are shaped with a small topknot. I prefer to cook brioche in bread pans as it makes them much easier to slice.

Serving Idea
Stale brioche is delicious for breakfast, lightly toasted and buttered. Top with your favorite preserves for a breakfast treat.

CROISSANTS

Croissants are not easy to make but are well worth the effort – the shaping is probably the easiest part of the whole process! We feel that an overnight rising and having the butter at the correct temperature are the keys to success.

MAKES 14

½ ounce compressed yeast
1¼ cups lukewarm water
4 cups bread flour or all-purpose flour
1 teaspoon salt
1 cup butter, softened at room temperature
1 egg, beaten

1. Crumble the yeast into the warm water and leave for 3-4 minutes, then stir to completely dissolve the yeast.

2. Mix the flour and salt in a bowl. Add the yeast liquid and mix to a smooth, stiff dough. Knead for 10 minutes until smooth and elastic then place in a bowl, cover and refrigerate overnight.

3. Knock back the dough and roll it out into a rectangle about 18 x 10 inches. Spread the butter out on two-thirds of the dough – if the butter is on the firm side, roll it out between two pieces of plastic wrap. Begin the layering process by folding the dough into three layers (a gatefold – see introduction).

4. Rest the dough for 10 minutes then repeat the rolling out and folding after turning the dough through 90 degrees. Repeat the whole process six times. Try to avoid the butter breaking through the surface of the dough and refrigerate for some of the resting periods.

5. Flour two baking sheets. Roll the dough out very thinly into a large rectangle a little bigger than 12 inches wide and 24 inches long. Trim the edges then cut in half lengthwise into two strips. Cut each strip into seven equal-sided triangles.

6. Shape the croissants by stretching the base of the triangles slightly and stretching the top away from you (see introduction), being careful not to tear the dough. Roll them up from the base, pressing lightly to keep the dough together. Curve the ends downwards as you transfer them to the baking sheets. Cover and leave to proof for 30 minutes, until slightly puffy.

7. Glaze the croissants well with the egg, without painting over the cut edges. Bake in a preheated 400°F oven for 15-20 minutes until golden. Cool briefly on a wire rack before serving.

Step 3 Roll the butter out between two pieces of plastic wrap if it is too firm.

Step 5 Cut each strip of dough into seven equal-sided triangles.

Cook's Notes

Time
Preparation takes about 20 minutes plus overnight rising, then another 2½ hours the next morning. Cooking takes 15-20 minutes.

Cook's Tip
Place the dough in a floured plastic bag for each resting period during the rolling and folding process, to prevent the dough from drying out.

Variation
To make savory croissants, place a slice of ham on each dough triangle, divide 1 cup grated Gruyère cheese between them and roll up.

PAIN AU CHOCOLAT

I think there is never enough chocolate in the pain au chocolat that you buy in the stores. Use a reasonable quality chocolate for the filling – we use chocolate pieces, to spread the filling throughout the pastries.

MAKES 10

½ ounce compressed yeast
1¼ cups lukewarm water
4 cups bread flour or all-purpose flour
1 teaspoon salt
1 cup butter, softened
⅔ cup semisweet chocolate pieces
Beaten egg for glazing
Superfine sugar to sprinkle

1. Crumble the yeast into the warm water and leave for 3-4 minutes. Mix the flour and salt together in a bowl and make a well in the center.

2. Stir the yeast to make sure that it is completely dissolved, then add the liquid to the flour and mix to form a firm dough.

3. Turn onto a floured surface and knead for about 10 minutes until smooth and elastic. Return the dough to the bowl, cover and refrigerate overnight.

4. Try to ensure that the butter is not too hard and not too soft. Punch down the dough and roll it out into a rectangle about 18 x 10 inches. Spread the butter out on two-thirds of the dough and begin the layering process by folding the dough into three layers (a gatefold, see introduction).

5. Leave the dough to rest for 15-20 minutes, then repeat the rolling and folding process, turning the dough through 90 degrees each time. Repeat the resting and rolling six times until the butter and dough are thoroughly layered. Try to avoid the butter breaking through the surface of the dough if you can.

6. Flour two baking sheets. Roll the dough out very thinly into a rectangle 12 x 24 inches, then cut it into two

Step 7 Sprinkle chocolate pieces down the center of the dough. Then fold one side over.

long strips about 6 inches wide. Cut the dough into rectangles; you should get five out of each strip.

7. Sprinkle half the chocolate pieces over the middle third of the dough and fold one side over. Scatter on the rest of the chocolate pieces and fold the remaining dough over in a gatefold. Brush the edges of the dough with water to seal. Place the pastries on the baking sheets then cover and leave to proof for another 30 minutes.

8. Brush the pastries with beaten egg and sprinkle them with superfine sugar. Bake in a preheated 400°F oven for 15-20 minutes, until golden in color. Cool on a wire rack.

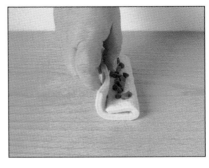

Step 7 Top with more chocolate pieces then fold the remaining dough over.

Cook's Notes

Preparation
Preparation takes about 20 minutes plus overnight rising, then another 3 hours the next morning. Cooking takes 15-20 minutes.

Cook's Tip
Seal the gatefold after filling the pastries firmly, or they may "unwrap" during cooking.

Watchpoint
Do not be tempted to eat the pastries immediately they are cooked as the chocolate pieces retain the heat.

DANISH PASTRIES

The secret of really good Danish pastries is to add a tiny pinch of ground cardamom.

MAKES 14 PASTRIES

¾ ounce compressed yeast
1 cup mixed lukewarm milk and water
2 tablespoons butter
4 cups all-purpose flour
Pinch of salt
Pinch of ground cardamom
1 egg plus 1 egg yolk
Grated rind of 1 lemon
1 cup less 2 tablespoons butter, softened

Custard filling
2 large eggs, beaten
¼ cup superfine sugar
¼ cup cornstarch
1¼ cups milk

Glaze
6 tablespoons apricot jam
¼ cup water

1. Crumble the yeast into the milk and water, leave for 3-4 minutes then stir until the yeast is dissolved.

2. Cut the butter into the flour and salt in a large bowl, then add the cardamom, eggs and lemon rind. Pour in the yeast liquid, mix to a firm, manageable dough. Turn

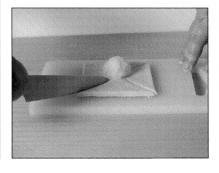

Step 6 Spoon some filling into the center of each square and cut the dough from the filling to the corners.

Step 6 Fold alternate corners up to the custard and press them down lightly to form pinwheels.

out onto a lightly floured surface and knead lightly. Place in a bowl, cover and refrigerate for 4-6 hours, or overnight.

3. Roll out the dough to a rectangle about 15 x 8 inches and spread the butter over it. Roll and fold the dough six times using the bookfold (see introduction) and rest the dough for 10-15 minutes in the refrigerator between each rolling.

4. To make the filling, whip the eggs and sugar with the cornstarch. Bring the milk to a boil in a saucepan and pour it onto the egg mixture, whisking constantly. Return to the pan and stir over the heat until thickened. Leave to cool.

5. Roll out the dough into a rectangle about 18 x 10 inches. Cut in half lengthwise then cut into 14 squares.

6. Spoon some custard into the middle of each square and cut the dough from the filling to the corners. Fold alternate corners up to the custard and press them down lightly. Place on floured baking sheets and leave covered for 20-30 minutes, until puffy.

7. Bake the pastries in a preheated 425°F oven for about 20 minutes, until golden brown. Prepare the glaze by boiling the jam and water for 3 minutes. Brush over the pastries as soon as they come out of the oven. Cool on a wire rack.

Cook's Notes

Time
Preparation takes about 20 minutes plus overnight rising, then about another 1½ hours the next morning. Cooking takes 20 minutes.

Variation
Use almond paste in place of custard for the filling. Drizzle the pastries with powdered sugar icing for a really professional finish.

Cook's Tip
Do not be tempted to substitute margarine for the butter as the end results will be heavier and have an inferior flavor.

SWEET PUMPKIN BREAD

This is a good loaf for afternoon tea or coffee, moist and delicious with preserves or just plain with butter.

MAKES 1 LARGE OR 2 SMALL LOAVES

¾ ounce compressed yeast
1 cup lukewarm water
6 cups bread flour or all-purpose flour
½ teaspoon salt
¼ cup superfine sugar
1¼ cups pumpkin purée
1 cup pitted dates, chopped
1 large egg, beaten

1. Crumble the yeast into the warm water and leave for 3-4 minutes, then stir to completely dissolve the yeast.

2. Mix together the flour, salt and sugar in a bowl, then make a well in the center and add the pumpkin purée.

3. Add the yeast liquid to the bowl, mixing the ingredients together into a soft but manageable dough.

4. Knead the dough for about 10 minutes on a lightly floured surface, until smooth and elastic. Return the dough to the bowl, cover and leave in a warm place for about 1 hour, until doubled in bulk.

5. Punch the dough down then work in the dates. Shape the dough and place in 1 large or 2 small oiled bread pans. Cover and leave to rise for another 30-40 minutes.

Step 2 Add the pumpkin purée to the flour.

6. Brush the loaves with the beaten egg and bake in a preheated 425°F oven for 35-40 minutes. Turn out onto a wire rack to cool. Serve sliced and buttered.

Step 5 Shape the dough then place it in the prepared bread pans.

Cook's Notes

Time
Preparation takes 2¼-2½ hours, cooking takes 35-40 minutes.

Cook's Tip
Scatter the dates over the whole of the dough to ensure that they are evenly distributed in the finished bread.

Variation
Add a little pumpkin pie spice to the flour before mixing.

LARDY CAKE

Definitely not recommended in the current healthy eating guidelines this traditional
English cake remains, nevertheless, one of our favorite cakes.

MAKES 1 LOAF

½ ounce compressed yeast
1¼ cups lukewarm milk
4 cups bread flour or all-purpose flour
1 teaspoon salt
1 tablespoon oil
¼ cup butter
¼ cup lard
¼ cup each currants and golden raisins
½ cup superfine sugar
1 teaspoon pumpkin pie spice

1. Crumble the yeast into the warm milk, leave for 3-4 minutes then stir to completely dissolve the yeast.

2. Mix the flour and salt together and make a well in the center. Add the oil and the yeast liquid and mix to a soft but manageable dough.

3. Turn out onto a floured surface and knead thoroughly until smooth and elastic. Return the dough to the bowl, cover and leave in a warm place for ¾-1 hour, until doubled in bulk.

4. Punch the dough down then roll it out into a rectangle about ½-inch thick. Dot half the butter and lard over two thirds of the dough, then cover it with half the fruits, sugar and spice.

5. Fold the dough using a gatefold (see introduction) then give the dough a quarter turn and repeat the rolling process, adding the remaining fats, fruit, sugar and spice. Repeat the gatefold then give the dough another quarter turn.

6. Roll out the dough to fit a rectangular 10 x 8-inch, or 9-inch square baking pan. Press the dough out to fill the corners of the pan then cover and leave for 30 minutes or until well risen.

7. Slash the top of the lardy cake in a diamond pattern using a sharp knife, then sprinkle a little extra sugar over the dough. Bake in a preheated 425°F oven for 30 minutes, then cool on a wire rack.

Step 4 Dot half the butter and lard over two thirds of the dough, then cover with half the fruits, sugar and spice.

Step 5 Fold the dough using a gatefold.

Cook's Notes

Time
Preparation takes 2-2½ hours, cooking takes 30 minutes.

Cook's Tip
Never cut this dough to fit a pan – all the filling will ooze out of the layers if you do. Try to prevent the fruit from breaking through the dough as this will also allow some of the fat to escape.

BARA BRITH

This traditional Welsh tea loaf was baked for special occasions.
It is very heavily fruited and we prefer to add the fruit after the kneading and then
to shape the loaf immediately, so that it only has one long rising.

MAKES 1 LARGE LOAF

3 cups bread flour or all-purpose flour
1 teaspoon salt
2 tablespoons butter
2 tablespoons superfine sugar
½ teaspoon pumpkin pie spice
1 ounce compressed yeast
⅔ cup lukewarm water
1 large egg, beaten
1¾ cups dried fruits (currants, raisins and golden raisins)
¼ cup candied peels
Beaten egg and superfine sugar for topping

Step 6 Brush the loaf with beaten egg then sprinkle with superfine sugar.

1. Place the flour and salt in a mixing bowl then cut in the butter. Stir in the sugar and spice.

2. Crumble the yeast into the warm water and leave for 2-3 minutes. Stir well to completely dissolve the yeast,

Step 2 Add the yeast liquid to the bowl with the beaten egg.

then add the liquid to the bowl with the beaten egg.

3. Mix to a soft but not sticky dough, then turn out onto a floured surface and knead thoroughly until smooth and elastic.

4. Gently work the fruits and peels into the dough – this takes some time as there is a lot of fruit.

5. Shape the dough into an oval and place it either on a floured baking sheet or in an oiled 8½ x 4½ x 2½-inch bread pan. Cover and leave to rise for about 1½ hours, until doubled in bulk.

6. Brush the loaf with beaten egg and sprinkle lightly with extra superfine sugar. Bake in a preheated 350°F oven for 35 minutes, then cool on a wire rack. Serve sliced and buttered.

Cook's Notes

Time
Preparation takes about 2 hours, cooking takes 35 minutes.

Cook's Tip
It is inevitable that some fruit will break through the surface of this loaf during kneading, but do try to keep this to a minimum.

BATH BUNS

These yeasted buns are named for the famous English west country spa town.

MAKES 18

4 cups bread flour or all-purpose flour
⅔ cup milk
¼ cup water
1 ounce compressed yeast
1 teaspoon salt
¼ cup superfine sugar
2 large eggs
¼ cup butter
1 cup golden raisins
⅓ cup candied peels
Beaten egg and granulated sugar for topping

1. Place 1 cup of the flour in a mixing bowl. Heat the milk and water together until lukewarm then crumble the yeast into the liquid and leave for 2-3 minutes. Stir well to completely dissolve the yeast, then add the liquid to the flour in the bowl. Mix well, cover and leave to rise in a warm place for about 20 minutes, until frothy.

2. Mix together the remaining flour, salt and sugar. Beat the eggs and melt the butter. Add all these ingredients to the fermented mixture along with the golden raisins and candied peels and stir well.

3. Turn out onto a floured surface and knead, adding more flour if necessary, until a smooth dough is formed. Return the dough to the bowl, cover, and leave for about 1 hour, until doubled in bulk.

4. Punch the dough down and place it in spoonfuls on

Step 2 Add the flour to the ferment with the eggs, butter and fruit.

Step 5 Brush the buns with beaten egg, then sprinkle them with granulated sugar.

greased baking sheets. Leave in a warm place for another 30 minutes to rise again.

5. Brush the buns with some beaten egg and sprinkle granulated sugar over them. Bake in a preheated 375°F oven for about 15 minutes, until dark golden brown. Sprinkle them with a little more sugar after baking, then cool on a wire rack.

Cook's Notes

⏱ **Time**
Preparation takes about 2¼ hours, cooking takes about 15 minutes.

🍴 **Cook's Tip**
Do not make the mixture too wet or the finished buns will be very heavy.

CURRANT BREAD

This is a traditional English bread, made throughout the country and reflecting the English love of dried fruits.

MAKES 1 LARGE LOAF

4 cups bread flour or all-purpose flour
1 teaspoon salt
¼ cup butter
2 tablespoons superfine sugar
¾ ounce compressed yeast
¾ cup lukewarm water
1 large egg, beaten
1⅓ cups currants
Beaten egg for glazing

1. Place the flour and salt in a bowl, cut in the butter, then stir in the sugar.

2. Crumble the yeast into the warm water and leave for 2-3 minutes, then stir well to completely dissolve the yeast. Add it to the flour with the beaten egg, and mix to form a soft dough.

3. Turn onto a lightly floured surface and knead the dough until smooth and elastic.

4. Return the dough to the bowl, cover and leave in a warm place for about 1 hour, until doubled in bulk.

5. Knock the dough back, then work in the currants.

6. Shape into a round loaf and place on a lightly floured baking sheet. Cover and leave to rise for another 30 minutes, until almost doubled in bulk.

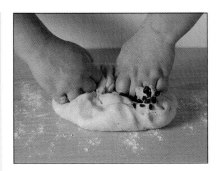
Step 5 Work in the currants.

Step 7 Brush the loaf with beaten egg.

7. Brush the loaf with some beaten egg, then bake in a preheated 425°F oven for 30 minutes. Cool on a wire rack before slicing and serving buttered.

Cook's Notes

Time
Preparation takes about 2 hours, cooking takes 30 minutes.

Cook's Tip
Work the currants carefully into the dough – if you overknead the dough will discolor.

CHELSEA BUNS

These buns are similar to Sticky Buns. They are kept moist and light by
baking them in a pan so that they join together. To serve, just pull a portion off. We like
lemon icing on our Chelsea buns, so the recipe for that is included too.

MAKES 12 BUNS

Buns
½ ounce compressed yeast
½ cup lukewarm milk
2 cups bread flour or all-purpose flour
½ teaspoon salt
1 tablespoon butter
1 large egg, beaten
1 tablespoon melted butter
⅔ cup mixed dried fruits (currants, raisins, golden
   raisins and candied peels)
¼ cup (firmly packed) brown sugar

Icing
½-⅔ cup powdered sugar
Juice of ½ lemon

1. Crumble the yeast into the warm milk in a mixing
bowl and leave for 3-4 minutes. Add ½ cup of the flour
and blend together until smooth. Cover and leave in a
warm place for 10-20 minutes, until the mixture froths.

2. Mix the remaining flour with the salt and cut in the
butter. Mix into the batter with the beaten egg and bring
together into a dough.

3. Turn onto a lightly floured surface and knead for
about 5 minutes. Return the dough to the bowl, cover
and leave in a warm place for 1-1½ hours, until doubled
in bulk. Lightly butter an 8-inch square cake pan.

4. Punch the dough down and roll it out into a rectangle
about 12 x 9 inches. Brush the dough with the melted
butter then cover it with the dried fruit and brown sugar.

5. Roll the dough up like a jelly roll, starting at one of
the longer sides. Cut into 12 equal slices and place
them, cut-side down, in the prepared cake pan. Cover
the pan and leave in a warm place for about 30
minutes, until the dough feels springy.

6. Bake the buns in a preheated 375°F oven for 30
minutes, then cool on a wire rack. Prepare the icing by
gradually working the sugar into the lemon juice to give
a thick but spoonable paste. Spoon some icing over
each bun, then leave until set.

Step 4 Brush the
dough with melted
butter then cover it
with the dried fruits
and brown sugar.

Step 5 Place the
buns in the prepared
cake pan.

Cook's Notes

⏲ Time
Preparation takes about 2½
hours, cooking takes 30 minutes.

Variation
Omit the icing and brush the
cooked buns with honey as soon as
they are baked.

Cook's Tip
Use a dough cutter to slice the
dough cleanly and evenly.

STICKY BUNS

These buns, a Philadelphia favorite, are based on an Amish recipe. They are also known as Cinnamon Rolls, or Cinnamon Snails (from *Schneken*, the Amish name for the dish) but whatever the name, they are delicious.

MAKES 14-16

Buns
1 ounce compressed yeast
¼ cup lukewarm water
¾ cup lukewarm milk
½ cup butter, softened
½ cup brown sugar
2 egg yolks
4 cups bread flour or all-purpose flour
1 teaspoon ground cinnamon
1 teaspoon salt
½ cup currants

Glaze
¼ cup water
2 tablespoons butter
¾ cup (firmly packed) brown sugar

1. Crumble the yeast into the warm water in a large mixing bowl and leave for about 5 minutes. Stir until dissolved then add the milk, butter, sugar and egg yolks followed by the flour, cinnamon and salt.

2. Mix well then knead the dough in the bowl until

Step 5 Sprinkle the currants over the syrup glaze.

Step 6 Arrange the buns on the top of the remaining glaze in the cake pan.

smooth. The dough will still be very sticky. Cover the bowl and leave for about 1 hour in a warm place, until the dough has doubled in bulk.

3. To prepare the glaze, place the water, butter and sugar in a saucepan and stir over a low heat until the sugar and butter have dissolved and melted. Butter a 10-inch shallow cake pan.

4. Punch the dough down on a floured work surface, then roll it into a rectangle about 12 inches long and ½-inch thick.

5. Carefully pour about half the glaze over the surface of the dough and sprinkle the currants evenly over the top. Quickly roll up the dough like a jelly roll, starting from one of the long sides, and cut it crosswise into 14-16 slices.

6. Pour the rest of the glaze into the buttered pan and arrange the buns on top. Cover and leave in a warm place to rise, about 20 minutes.

7. Bake the buns in a preheated 375°F oven for about 30 minutes or until they are well browned on top. Turn out onto a wire rack and leave the buns sticky-side upward to cool.

Cook's Notes

Time
Preparation takes about 2 hours, cooking takes 30 minutes.

Preparation
This dough is very soft and difficult to manage, but do persevere as the buns are delicious.

Cook's Tip
Use a dough cutter to slice the dough cleanly and evenly.

HOT CROSS BUNS

These English yeasted buns, richly spiced and fruited, are traditionally eaten at Easter. We have developed a new custom in our village – we visit our friends with homemade hot cross buns on Good Friday morning. If we catch them off guard they sometimes give us their Easter eggs in exchange!

MAKES 12

Buns
1 ounce compressed yeast
⅔ cup lukewarm milk
2 cups bread flour or all-purpose flour
1¾ cups whole-wheat flour
½ teaspoon salt
1 teaspoon grated nutmeg
1 teaspoon pumpkin pie spice
1 teaspoon ground cinnamon
6 tablespoons superfine sugar
6 tablespoons butter
1 large egg, beaten
⅓ cup each currants, golden raisins and candied peels

Paste
¼ cup butter
1 cup all-purpose flour
½ cup water

Glaze
3 tablespoons superfine sugar
3 tablespoons each milk and water

Step 5 Cut a cross in the top of each bun with a sharp knife.

Step 5 Pipe a cross of paste over each cut.

1. Crumble the yeast into the warm milk and leave for 3-4 minutes, then stir to dissolve the yeast completely.

2. Mix the flours, salt, spices and sugar in a large bowl, then cut in the butter. Add the egg and the yeast liquid and mix to a soft but manageable dough.

3. Turn the dough out onto a floured surface and knead thoroughly until smooth and elastic. Return to the bowl, cover and refrigerate overnight.

4. Punch the dough down, then work in the fruit and peels. Divide into 12 pieces and shape into buns. Place on a floured baking sheet, cover and leave in a warm place for 30 minutes, until well risen.

5. Prepare the paste by beating the butter and flour together and then working in the water to make a thick paste. Place in a pastry bag fitted with a ¼-inch plain, round tip. Cut a cross in the top of each bun then pipe a cross of paste over the cuts. Bake in a preheated 425°F oven for 20-25 minutes.

6. Meanwhile, prepare the glaze. Gently heat the sugar, milk and water until the sugar has dissolved, then boil rapidly for about 2 minutes to make a thick syrup. Transfer the buns to a wire rack and brush them immediately with the glaze.

Cook's Notes

Time
Preparation takes about 20 minutes plus overnight rising, then about another 45 minutes the next day. Cooking takes 20-25 minutes.

Cook's Tip
This generous quantity of paste allows plenty to pipe really pronounced crosses on the buns.

Preparation
If the dough is a bit dry when mixing, add a little extra warm water.

PANETTONE

This is a traditional Italian Christmas bread, often served at breakfast time with jam. Choose top quality fruits and peel and you will be well rewarded by the delicious flavor of this bread.

MAKES 1 LOAF

1½ ounces compressed yeast
Scant ¼ cup lukewarm water
6 egg yolks
1 tablespoon vanilla extract
Grated rind of 1 lemon
½ teaspoon salt
¼ cup superfine sugar
2 cups bread flour or all-purpose flour
½ cup butter, softened at room temperature
⅓ cup good quality candied peels, finely chopped
½ cup golden raisins or raisins
2 tablespoons unsalted butter, melted

1. Crumble the yeast into the water and leave for 5 minutes before stirring to completely dissolve the yeast. Leave in a warm place for 10-15 minutes.

2. Scrape the yeast liquid into a large bowl and add the egg yolks, vanilla, lemon rind, salt and sugar. Add the flour gradually, beating all the time, until the dough is soft and sticky but can be gathered together in a ball.

3. Add the softened butter in three large pieces and work it into the dough – the mixture will become very

Step 3 Add the softened butter in three large pieces.

Step 6 Press the dough into an oiled bread pan.

heavy and sticky as the butter becomes incorporated. Add just a little more flour if absolutely necessary, then knead for a good 10 minutes, until smooth and shiny.

4. Put the dough in a lightly floured bowl. Cover and leave in a warm place until doubled in bulk – this will take about 2 hours, because the mixture is so rich.

5. Scrape the mixture out of the bowl onto a lightly floured surface and knock back gently. Flatten out the dough, add the peels and fruits and knead until they are evenly incorporated. Try to prevent the fruits from breaking through the top crust of the dough.

6. Lightly oil an 8½ x 4½ x 2½-inch bread pan, press the dough into it and leave for another 45 minutes, until risen to the top of the pan.

7. Carefully brush the panettone with a little of the melted butter, then bake in a preheated 400°F oven for 10 minutes. Reduce the temperature to 350°F and bake for 30 minutes, until dark golden brown. Brush the loaf once or twice with the melted butter during cooking. Cool in the pan for a few minutes then turn out onto a wire rack to cool completely.

Cook's Notes

Time
Preparation takes about 3½-3¾ hours, cooking takes 40 minutes.

Cook's Tip
The mixing and kneading process is easiest done in an electric mixer.

Serving Idea
Serve sliced with preserves and strong coffee or a well-chilled dessert wine.

ALMOND PASTE COFFEE CAKE

This yeasted cake, called a tea ring in Britain, is traditionally served at Christmas and on other festive occasions, but we think any celebration is a good excuse to indulge.

MAKES 1

½ ounce compressed yeast
6 tablespoons lukewarm milk
2 cups bread flour or all-purpose flour
Pinch of salt
¼ cup superfine sugar
6 tablespoons butter
1 large egg, beaten
3 tablespoons sieved apricot preserves
⅓ cup chopped candied peels
4 ounces almond paste
1 large egg, beaten

Powdered sugar icing
Scant 1 cup sifted powdered sugar
Juice of ½ lemon
2-3 tablespoons slivered almonds, toasted

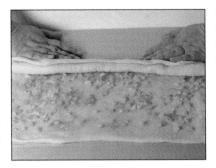

Step 5 Roll up the dough, enclosing the almond paste and peel.

Step 7 Slash the dough across the ring.

1. Crumble the yeast into the warm milk and leave for 3-4 minutes, then stir until completely dissolved.

2. Mix the flour, salt and sugar in a bowl, then cut in ¼ cup of the butter. Make a well in the center, add the egg and yeast liquid and mix to a soft, manageable dough.

3. Turn out onto a lightly floured surface and knead thoroughly until smooth and elastic. Return the dough to the bowl, cover and leave in a warm place for about 1 hour, until doubled in bulk. Melt the remaining butter.

4. Knock back the dough then roll it out into a rectangle about 16 x 12 inches. Brush with the melted butter and preserves, then scatter over the candied peels.

5. Form the almond paste into a roll the same length as the dough and place it along the dough. Roll the dough

up and seal the edge with some of the beaten egg.

6. Shape into a ring on a floured baking sheet, sealing the ends together with more egg. Cover and leave for 30-45 minutes in a warm place, until well risen.

7. Brush the ring with the remaining egg then slash the dough across the ring. Bake in a preheated 400°F oven for 30-35 minutes, then cool on a wire rack.

8. Mix the powdered sugar with sufficient lemon juice to give a thick, spoonable icing. Drizzle it over the cake and decorate with the almonds. Leave to set before serving sliced.

Cook's Notes

Time
Preparation takes about 2½ hours, cooking takes 30-35 minutes.

Variation
Omit the almond paste and add some golden raisins with the peels.

STOLLEN

This is a traditional festive bread, popular in Germany and throughout Northern Europe. We like our Stollens to contain almond paste. Plainer varieties are sometimes buttered.

MAKES 2 LOAVES

1 ounce compressed yeast
⅔ cup lukewarm milk
¼ ounce superfine sugar
4 cups bread flour or all-purpose flour
Pinch of salt
3 tablespoons brown sugar
¼ cup butter
2 large eggs, beaten
1 tablespoon rum
⅓ cup each currants, raisins and golden raisins
Grated rind of ½ lemon
4 ounces almond paste
Powdered sugar to decorate

1. Crumble the yeast into the warm milk, leave for 3-4 minutes then stir until completely dissolved. Add the superfine sugar and 1 cup of the flour and mix well. Cover and leave for about 1 hour until the mixture becomes frothy.

2. Add the remaining flour, the salt, brown sugar, 6 tablespoons of the butter, half the egg and the rum and mix well to form a manageable dough. Knead on a floured surface until it becomes smooth and elastic. Cover and leave to rise for about 1 hour, until doubled in bulk.

3. Punch the dough down and add the dried fruit and the lemon rind. Do not knead too much at this stage, but try to ensure that the fruit is evenly distributed.

4. Divide the dough into two pieces and shape into ovals. Make an indentation lengthwise, towards the bottom of each oval. Roll the almond paste out into two

Step 4 Make an indentation lengthwise towards the bottom of each oval.

equal-sized pieces, the same length as the dough. Place the almond paste in the indentations and fold the dough towards you, sealing the edges with some of the remaining beaten egg. Cover the stollens and leave to rise for another 20-30 minutes.

5. Brush the stollen with more beaten egg and bake in a preheated 350°F oven for 30 minutes or until they are golden brown.

6. Cool the stollens on a wire rack. Melt the remaining butter and brush it over the cooled loaves, then sprinkle them with some sifted powdered sugar.

Step 4 Fold the dough towards you over the almond paste, then seal the edges with beaten egg.

Cook's Notes

Time
Preparation takes about 2¾ hours, cooking takes 30 minutes.

Preparation
Do not place the almond paste right on the fold of the stollen, or the loaf may spring open during proofing or baking.

Cook's Tip
If wrapped decoratively, these loaves make a lovely Christmas present for foodie friends.

SAVARIN

This rich yeast cake, baked in a ring, is brushed with syrup and then filled with fresh fruits to make an elegant dessert.

MAKES 1

1 ounce compressed yeast
6 tablespoons warm milk
2 cups bread flour or all-purpose flour
½ teaspoon salt
2 tablespoons superfine sugar
4 large eggs, beaten
½ cup unsalted butter, softened

Syrup
½ cup clear honey
½ cup water
2-3 tablespoons rum

Fresh fruits to serve

1. Crumble the yeast into the warm milk in a large bowl and leave for 3-4 minutes, then stir until the yeast has completely dissolved. Add 3 tablespoons of the flour and leave covered in a warm place for 20 minutes, until slightly frothy.

2. Add the remaining flour, the salt, sugar, eggs and softened butter and beat for 3-4 minutes in the bowl.

3. Lightly oil a 10-inch tube pan and spoon the batter evenly into it. Cover and leave in a warm place for about 40 minutes, until the dough has risen almost to the top of the pan.

4. Bake the savarin in a preheated 400°F oven for 40 minutes, or until shrinking away from the edges of the pan. Prepare the rum syrup while the savarin is baking. Boil the honey and water together until slightly thickened, then add the rum.

5. Turn the savarin out onto a wire rack and brush with the rum syrup while still hot. Brush repeatedly until all the syrup is used up and the savarin is well moistened, then leave it to cool completely. Fill the center with fresh fruits in season before serving.

Step 2 Add the remaining flour with the salt, sugar, eggs and softened butter.

Step 3 Spoon the dough into an oiled tube pan.

Cook's Notes

Time
Preparation takes about 1½ hours, cooking takes about 40 minutes.

Variation
Add ¾ cup currants to the dough and bake in small round molds or greased muffin pans to make rum babas.

Serving Idea
Serve with whipped cream or crème fraîche.

Index